Breaking Tradition
THE STORY OF
LOUISE NEVELSON

Books by Natalie S. Bober

A RESTLESS SPIRIT:
The Story of Robert Frost

BREAKING TRADITION:
The Story of Louise Nevelson

Breaking Tradition

THE STORY
OF
LOUISE
NEVELSON

by Natalie S. Bober

Atheneum · 1984 · New York

Frontis

Smithsonian Institution. PHOTOGRAPH BY RENATE PONSOLD.

Excerpts from *Dawns and Dusks: Louise Nevelson,* by Diana MacKown
are reprinted with the permission of Charles Scribner's Sons.
Copyright © 1976 by Diana MacKown.

Library of Congress Cataloging in Publication Data

Bober, Natalie S.   *Breaking tradition.*

Summary: A *biography of the woman considered by many to be the*
finest living American artist of our time.
1. Nevelson, Louise, 1900–   —Juvenile literature.   2. Sculptors—
United States—Biography—Juvenile literature.   [1. Nevelson, Louise,
1900–   . 2. Sculptors]   I. Title.
NB237.N43B62   1984   730'.92'4 [B] [92]   83-15618
ISBN 0-689-31036-6

Contents

Acknowledgements

SO MANY PEOPLE were helpful at the various stages in my research and writing that it seems fitting that I express publicly my gratitude to those who played an important role in the shaping of the book.

Roberta Payne, Children's Librarian at the Metropolitan Museum of Art in New York, first spoke to me of the need for a biography of Louise Nevelson. Charles Diker made the initial introduction to Mrs. Nevelson.

Linda and David Gordon merit a special vote of thanks for their part in it.

Elizabeth Bettcher, Nevelson Archivist, and Christine Podmaniczky, Curator, at the Farnsworth Library and Art Museum in Rockland, Maine were particularly helpful, devoting much time and effort to my project. To them, and to May Castlebury, Librarian at the Whitney Museum of American Art in New York; Elyse Quasbarth and Sheila Hoban, Photo Archivist, at the Archives of American Art in Washington, D.C.; Ann Shorin, Chairman of the Board, and Constance Schwartz, Curator, of the Nassau County Museum of Fine Art in Roslyn, N.Y.; Nancy Kessler-Post, Librarian, Museum of the City of New York; Suzanne Landau, Curator of Contemporary Art, Israel Museum, Jerusalem; Gloria Block of the New York office of the Museum of the Diaspora, Israel; Stephanie Stern of the Leo Baeck Institute in New York; Dina Abramowicz of YIVO Institute for Jewish Studies in New York; and Rabbi Bernard H. Mehlman of Temple Israel in Boston, my gratitude for all their efforts on my behalf.

To dear friend Phillip Goldfein for his interest and enthusiasm, and for introducing me to Rabbi Gilbert Rosenthal; and to Rabbi Rosenthal, for his patient explanation of the teachings of the *Talmud* and his careful documenting of the specific tractate that was so significant in the life of Louise Nevelson, my thanks and my appreciation.

I am deeply indebted to Phyllis Coniglio, whose help at a crucial moment became for me a lee port in a storm, and to Steven Samuels who once again offered advice and encouragement.

A very special debt of gratitude is owed to Anita Weinstein for the reminiscences of her childhood that she so graciously shared with me; to Louise Nevelson for access to archival material and to restricted interviews, and for the great gift of her time; to my editor, Marcia Marshall, who early on caught my enthusiasm for Louise Nevelson and made it possible for my dream to become a reality; and to Estelle Riback, treasured friend, art historian and sculptor in her own right, who acted as art consultant at various stages, reading and rereading the manuscript for accuracy.

To two very special people, Estelle Goodman and Dorothy Ehrich, whose devotion, meticulous attention to detail and mammoth job of assistance on the index would have pleased my mother; and to Dorothy Ehrich also for accompanying me to Washington, D.C. to sift through boxes and boxes of materials, offering thoughtful suggestions as well as moral support, my love and appreciation.

My daughter Betsy, whose editorial eye is far more astute than her mother's, and whose knowledge and love of art were my original inspiration, has, by her encouragement, creative ideas and hard work made it possible for me to keep alive the legacy of her grandmother. To her and to my husband Larry— for his interest and encouragement, for his magnificent photography, but mostly for the joy of sharing my work with him that "has made all the difference,"—my gratitude and my love. N.S.B.

Foreword

HISTORY WILL undoubtedly record Louise Nevelson as one of the greatest artists of her time, ranked, perhaps, with Picasso and Matisse. At present, at the age of eighty-four, she is considered by many in the art world to be the finest living American artist—this, unqualified by either the word *woman* or the word *sculptor*. But of the many young people who recognize her photograph instantly in a newspaper or magazine article, few can connect her with her work. Her striking appearance—the long eyelashes, the assemblage of clothes, the scarf invariably wrapped around her head—are quickly identified. Yet she is, as Edward Albee has called her, ". . . a bird of rare plumage . . . whose art and persona are perhaps more the same thing—in the very best of senses—than any other living artist."

While there are several beautiful books available for the art connoisseur that depict her art, there is no definitive biography of her for the young adult. Roberta Payne, Children's Librarian at the Metropolitan Museum of Art in New York, cites this as a particularly troubling void.

I have attempted to fill that void. But I have *not* attempted to interpret or to criticize the art of Louise Nevelson. (All the references to interpretation or criticism of her art by qualified experts have been carefully documented. And Diana MacKown's superb book, *Dawns + Dusks*, served as an invaluable guide throughout the entire period of research and writing.) A lifelong interest in the creative arts, a strong background in the humanities, and many years of teaching have prompted me to tell the stories of men and women whose artistic achievements might serve as an inspiration for students. A special attraction to the sculpture of Louise Nevelson led to investigation into the life that produced that work.

Thus, I have attempted here to describe Louise Nevelson—the milieu from which she sprang, the forces that shaped her life, and the way in which her art was an outgrowth of that life. She long ago made the choice to dedicate her life to art. She had the courage to make that choice. The strength came from her belief in herself. She knew what she had. She made it a reality.

> *Who is an artist? I say we take a title.*
> *No one gives it to us. We make our lives.*

Nevelson's perseverance in the face of seemingly insurmountable hardships and the eventual total freedom that grew out of them, her independence, her philosophy of life and her strong sense of self ("You belong to yourself. . . . you can only be a total human being to others when you know who you are.") make her an appealing subject for anyone interested in the arts, in creating, in simply being a productive person in the eighties.

She is a romantic, intuitive, creative woman who has expressed the feeling that her "works are definitely feminine." Yet she has never felt that being a woman was a handicap. To her, ability is what counts. "Let's break tradition," she has said. This she has done—brilliantly—in her art and in her life. It is my hope that her story will serve as an inspiration to young people everywhere.   N.S.B.

For
the memory of my mother
and for
my husband and my daughter
who have helped me keep
a legacy alive

To recall the destruction of the Temple in Jerusalem, the sages ordained that when a person builds a house, a small section should be left unfinished.

Babylonian Talmud
Baba Batra 6ob

Jars of Colored Candy

LOUISE AWOKE and immediately sensed the excitement running through the ship like electricity.

We must be there! she thought.

As she peered out the porthole, she saw, for the first time, the sun rising over Penobscot Bay. In the early morning light she could distinguish the silhouettes of the sailboats in the harbor and the bustle of activity that was just beginning on the dock.

At her mother's urging, she washed quickly at the big copper wash bowl, luxuriating for a moment in the wonder of running water, then dressed in the Persian lamb coat and hat her mother had brought with them from Russia, and ran up on deck with her brother and sister.

Louise Berliawsky was only five, but she was tall for her age, and beautiful, with her long dark hair and rosy complexion. Her sister Anita, not quite three, followed Louise everywhere. Nathan, at seven the oldest of the children, was already protective of his younger sisters.

The year was 1905, and the children and their mother, Minna, had just made the long and difficult journey across the Atlantic Ocean from Russia. They had landed in Boston, Massachusetts, and were now completing the last leg of their trip—the boat ride from Boston to Rockland, Maine. Here they would join their father, Isaac, and begin a new life in America.

It was early spring and there was a chill in the air. The sun came up quickly and the sky was the deep, deep blue of Maine. The small sailboats and large three- and four-masted schooners already astir all around were a forecast of the activity that would mark this busy harbor in summer.

Now, as they stood on the deck, looking at the city that was to be their new home, the children saw the low buildings lining the waterfront and, in the distance, the smoke from the lime kilns rising above the town.

When the boat was finally docked at Tillson's Wharf, it was an anxious little band of weary travelers who disembarked and started up Tillson Avenue toward Sea Street— and the little house their father had secured for them in the poor waterfront area. As they looked ahead they could see Main Street with its electric, telephone, and trolley lines, and the strange-looking newly installed carbon arc electric street lights.

The people they saw lining the dock (townspeople always came down to greet the arrival of one of the steamships from Boston) or walking on Main Street were dressed very differently from the way they and their mother were dressed. They even spoke a strange language the newcomers didn't understand. Young as she was, Louise sensed that life here in America would be far different from the life she had known and loved on her grandparents' little farm in the tiny town of Shushneky, in Russia.

And she was not wrong. Rockland was an old New England Yankee town that boasted many wealthy families living in beautiful homes. It would not be warmly receptive to this newly-arrived immigrant Jewish family who spoke only Yiddish and Russian, dressed elaborately, and had a name like Berliawsky.

But Isaac Berliawsky had settled here two years before, and now he had earned enough money to send for his wife and three children. He still hoped, though, that some day they would be able to make their way to New York.

ISAAC had been born into an educated and prosperous family in the historic old city of Pereyaslav, very near Kiev, Russia, in the 1870s. (The cities of Kiev and Pereyaslav are both in the province of Kiev.) His father was the town scribe, an older brother was a student of the *Talmud*,* and the family was engaged in the lumber business and in the manufacture of vodka.

Kiev, on the Dnieper River, is at the crossroads of Western Europe and the Orient, and had always attracted Jewish settlers. At the time that Isaac lived there it had already become the economic and commercial center of the southwestern region of Russia.

But the tradition of hatred toward Jews had recently resurfaced there, and although Jews continued to play a significant role in the economy of all the area, they were not allowed to own land. Therefore, the Berliawsky's lumber business consisted of buying crops of trees, which they called "woods," then processing the lumber and transporting it.

In May of 1881, a pogrom (an organized massacre) took place in which Jewish houses and shops in Kiev were

* Collection of ancient Rabbinic writings that are the basis of Jewish traditional law

looted and burned, synagogues were desecrated, people were senselessly beaten or murdered, and hundreds of Jewish families were completely ruined. Shortly after this, and probably as a direct result of it, Isaac's brothers and sisters began emigrating to the United States and Canada. Isaac chose to remain at home to care for his parents and to work with his father.

The Berliawsky family owned "woods" outside of Kiev near the little town of Shushneky,* also on the Dnieper River. Occasionally Isaac had to go there to cut down trees or arrange to have the timber floated down the river from there.

Minna Ziesel Smolerank, unlike Isaac Berliawsky, had grown up in Sushneky. She was a poor farmer's daughter, attached to her family and content to live the life of the Jew in the shtetl.

A shtetl was very different from the great city of Pereyaslav that boasted wide cobblestone streets, wooden sidewalks, rooftops of tin, and brick shops with iron doors.

Shtetl is a Yiddish word that means small city, but the word conjures up a whole way of life. The warm and intimate life style of the shtetl was bound up with the traditional ideals of Judaism: piety, learning and scholarship, justice, and charity. Over all was a feeling of mutual interdependence—a responsibility of a community for the survival of its members. Here, in the world of the shtetl, Jews lived as an isolated group, dependent on one another.

A typical shtetl had unpaved streets and a jumble of wooden houses clustered around a teeming marketplace crowded with shops, booths, tables, stands, and butchers'

---

* Shushneky was little more than "a bend in the road," and its exact spelling can no longer be verified.

blocks. Here, while animals wandered freely about, Russian peasant women dressed in drab mended dresses, with a shawl over their shoulders and a basket on their arms— their money tied in a corner of a large handkerchief, would come every day to exchange their livestock, vegetables, freshly picked fruits and melons, and fish for dry goods, shirts, hats, shoes, lamps and oil.[1]

It was in such a market place in Shushneky that Isaac first saw Minna. And it was from here that she would ultimately be transplanted into the staid American seacoast town of Rockland, Maine.

One day, when Minna was just sixteen, she was walking in the marketplace when Isaac came riding into town on a white horse. He was tall and slim, with the unusual combination of fair skin and blue eyes set against jet black hair accentuating his aristocratic good looks. He saw Minna, was struck by her beauty, and immediately asked who she was and where she lived. He began to pursue her, soon fell in love with her, and insisted that she marry him.

Minna was attracted to this exciting and handsome young man, but she knew that she shouldn't marry him. She was much younger than he (he was already in his twenties), their backgrounds were different, and he was pursuing her too avidly. She was almost frightened by his persistence. So she decided to run away.

Her older sister lived in a little town on the other side of the Dnieper River. The river was only about five hundred yards wide at this point, and Minna knew that very soon it would freeze—as it always did at that time of year. Then she could walk across to the shelter of her sister's home, where Isaac wouldn't find her. The Dnieper, as are most Russian rivers, is iced over for eighty to one hundred twenty days every year.

She watched and waited impatiently for the weather to turn colder and the water to turn to ice. But this was the one year in a hundred that the river didn't freeze.

So Minna married Isaac and set about trying to be a proper wife. Isaac tried hard to please her. A year after they were married a son, Nathan, was born to them. Two years later, in September of 1899, Louise was born.* A second daughter, Anita, arrived in 1902. Just a short while after Anita was born, Isaac's father succumbed to the cancer that had been plaguing him.

Now, with his father gone, and all his brothers and sisters already in Canada or the United States, Isaac decided the time had come for him to go to America. There was no longer anything to keep him in Russia, and he was free to leave his homeland—to seek, as his brothers and sisters had, the freedom, the opportunities, the new modes of life available in the "golden land" to the west.

So he sent his wife and three small children back to her parents' home and set off for America. (His own mother would follow later, also.) He stayed briefly with a brother in Waterville, Maine, but soon realized that as long as he worked for his brother he could never have the independence he craved. So he boarded a train, gave the conductor all the money he had left in his pocket, and asked in his halting English to be let off when the money ran out. He got off in Rockland, Maine.

There he sought out the Rabbi in the town and accepted an invitation to stay in the Rabbi's home until he

* Russia adhered to the ancient calendar devised by Julius Caesar's Romans. That calendar was thirteen days behind the more commonly accepted one. Perhaps this is the reason that Louise is not certain of the exact date of her birthday. She celebrates it on September 23.

could earn some money and find a room to rent for him-self.[2]

————————————————

BACK IN RUSSIA, Louise, at three years old a shy and quiet little girl, suddenly stopped talking. For six months Minna feared her daughter had become deaf and dumb. But Louise was simply reacting to what she thought was desertion by the father she loved.

The two years that the family spent in Shushneky until Isaac was able to send for them were relatively calm ones. The children felt loved and protected by their grandpar-ents. They enjoyed the warmth and security of shtetl life. Louise particularly enjoyed watching her grandmother dye wool with the many colored vegetable dyes she used. She would carry the memory of these colors in her mind's eye for years afterward. She was already beginning to develop the visual mind that would lead her to art.

Sholom Aleichem, whose humorous tales of Jewish life in the shtetls of Eastern Europe were immortalized in *Fiddler on the Roof*, grew up in Pereyaslav. One of his sisters was a friend and neighbor of Minna's. One day, when Sholom Aleichem was visitng his sister, she invited Minna in to meet him. When he looked at Minna he told his sister, "She took her face from Heaven." Later, he said of little Louise, "She's destined for greatness." Minna would repeat this story to Louise years later.[3]

When Isaac finally earned enough money to send for his family, Minna was distraught. She was torn between love for her husband and her obligation to follow him to America with their children, and her reluctance to leave the parents she adored. She understood that she was relinquishing the support system of the shtetl and the protection of her parents, whom she would never see again, for a strange land and a strange culture.

With characteristic resolve and quiet strength, Minna packed their clothes, sold her remaining possessions, and explained to the children that they were about to embark on an adventure that would take them across the sea to a new country—and to their father. Only her eyes betrayed her sadness.

The trip—by wagon, train, and then by boat across the Atlantic Ocean—took several months and was not a pleasant one. On the boat the passengers were forced to huddle together in the cramped, dirty quarters of the steerage section, way down in the hold of the ship. Struggling for space, and unable to sleep in the narrow bunks, they could barely eat the food that was ladled from huge kettles into dinner pails and were often unable even to get a cupful of water. The memories of the constant noise of the steering mechanism and the engine, the foul smells, the seasickness all around her, the struggle to learn a few English words would stay with Louise forever.

But there was one bright spot in the trip for Louise— one that would make an indelible impression on her mind. It occurred when the boat made a stopover in Liverpool, England. Caught up in the excitement of the depot at Liverpool—of the lights, the incredible space after the confines of the boat, and the people moving about—Minna took the children into a candy shop. Here for the first time in their lives, they saw shelf upon shelf of glass jars, each filled with a different color of hard candy. The lights shining on them reflected a rainbow of color that, to the little girl of five, "looked like Heaven." Louise never forgot that sight.[4]

Then, when the children came down with measles they were all quarantined in Liverpool for six weeks. It was here that Louise, playing with one of the other children, first saw a doll. When the doll was laid down, its eyes would shut. Louise thought surely this was magic. Perhaps it was the memory of this that stimulated her interest in *surrealistic** art many years later. Today she still thinks that dolls are unique—almost surrealistic—and that trying to make a doll seem human imparts a mystical quality to it.[5]

———————◆◦◆◦◆———————

NOW the Berliawsky family was finally in America, in the seacoast town of Rockland, Maine. At the time, the United States was a young country rich in natural resources and opportunity, with Teddy Roosevelt as its president.

The many forests of Maine, with their seemingly inexhaustible stands of trees and thriving lumber industry helped the state to become one of the major shipbuilding centers of the country. And in Rockland, situated as it is on a fine harbor, shipbuilding, shipowning and seafaring had become a way of life.

The world's deepest lime quarries are also in Rockland, and the quarrying and burning of lime, begun there in the 1790s, helped it to become a major commercial port. For one hundred years New York, Boston, and other large cities depended on Rockland lime for use in the concrete to construct their buildings. This, in turn, created a need for ships to carry the lime to market.

* Surrealism was a movement in art and literature that was founded in Paris in 1924 by a French poet named André Breton. The surrealists invented the word to mean *super* realism. They declared that a magical world, more beautiful than the real world, can be created in art.

A 4,346-foot granite jetty was built by the United States government in the Rockland harbor between 1881 and 1899. With this, Rockland became the busiest port in the area and the focal point for wealthy families arriving by ship from Boston or New York on their way to summer holidays in Maine. Main Street in Rockland became a commercial center for New England, and the summer people always found time to stop into its shops which, even then, stocked the latest in New York fashions.

In this milieu Minna struggled to make a new life for herself and her family. She quickly set about creating a comfortable home for them. Even in the small, shabby old house, all was neat and made to shine. By fall, when Louise and Nate were ready to start school, they were all speaking English, and Minna was expecting another child.

When the baby was born—a little girl whom they named Lillian—Louise, not quite seven, suddenly stopped playing with dolls. She decided that she preferred her dark red monkey with its funny brown face and dragged it around with her wherever she went. She seemed to associate playing with dolls with taking care of her new baby sister. And she wanted no part of that.

Soon after, Isaac bought an old house on Linden Street, on the south side of town, overlooking the water, and moved his family there. Now the children would fall asleep at night and wake up each morning to the sound of the waves pounding against the rocks. During the day they played at the water's edge, collected driftwood that had been washed up onto the beach, or sat and watched the large wooden ships being built at the shipyard around the corner.

By this time Isaac had begun to work in real estate, contracting and building. When his wife and children had first arrived, he was still experiencing difficulty with the language and was uncertain which direction his life should take. He had felt, then, that Rockland was simply an interim step for them, until he could earn enough money to move his family to New York.

But soon he realized that in America he could buy land as his father had not been able to in Russia. With his understanding of the lumber business from his work with his father, he was able to own a lumber yard, build houses on his land, mortgage them, then use the money to buy more land, and repeat the process. Eventually, he would become the fourth highest taxpayer in Rockland. While he never became rich—all the property was mortgaged—he was a hard worker, fast, smart, and scrupulously honest, and he provided well for his family. He became a highly respected member of the community.[6]

LIFE in the Berliawsky household was peaceful and soon settled into a routine.

Generally, Isaac was the first to rise in the morning. By five o'clock he would begin to wake the children to come downstairs for the breakfast he had already prepared. The children didn't mind getting up so early because it was the one time of the day that they could snatch a few minutes to talk to him. Louise, particularly, treasured these early morning moments with her father.

Minna generally made lunch, the main meal of the day. Her recipes were limited, but whatever she did cook was delicious, and often Nate, Louise, and Anita would run all the way home from school—which was on the opposite side of town—in order to have time to enjoy their mother's lunch. They needed every minute of their lunch period to accomplish this, since the school was more than a mile away.

Louise loved this walk back and forth in the springtime when the rich green foliage of the trees lining their route seemed to her like umbrellas over their heads. Years later she would transfer this image to canvas.

Frequently, though, there were days when the children would come home from school, breathless from their long run, only to find their mother in bed with a severe backache or headache and weeping for her own mother, left behind in Russia. (Minna never seemed to adjust to life in Rockland and to the separation from her parents. She was often depressed and suffered from pain that doctors could neither diagnose nor cure.) On those days Louise made something cold and simple for all of them.

There was always plenty of food in the house. The children looked forward to the coming of the milkman, who delivered galvanized cans of cream for eight cents a quart from which Minna made sour cream and cheese. They waited also for the farmer who came to sell his products. There were always a barrel of potatoes, a case of eggs, and a bushel of apples in the basement.

Little Anita watched eagerly for the coming of the rag peddler. Of all the tradesmen, he was her favorite. Whenever he came he would take her for a ride in his cart, then put her on his knee and teach her to sing Russian songs. When she got a little older he taught her to count in Russian. Then she could show Louise that she knew Russian, too! Minna was only too glad to have her go. It got her out from underfoot for a while.[7]

Louise, on the other hand, never seemed to get in the

The Berliawsky family in Rockland, Maine, about 1908. Louise is at right. SMITHSONIAN INSTITUTION.

way. Whenever there was free time she would sit at the kitchen table and draw. Even before she was six she was drawing pictures that were being praised by her teachers and her family alike. Art was already becoming a happy part of her life.

One of her earliest memories of school is of the beautiful teacher who brought colored chalk into her classroom. Then, when Louise was in second grade, the art teacher, who came to school once a week, showed the boys and girls a crayoned drawing of a sunflower. She asked the children to look at it carefully and then reproduce it. Louise drew a large brown circle surrounded by tiny yellow petals. The teacher held it up to show the class. She called it the most *original* because Louise had altered the proportions of the flower. Louise didn't know what *original* meant, but she could sense that it was a "praise" word—and she was pleased.[8]

More and more Louise was finding that all she wanted to do was draw pictures. Anita, who was just learning to read, always had her head buried in a book, or would beg to be read to. But Louise never wanted to listen to the fairy tales her younger sisters enjoyed hearing, and certainly wouldn't pick up a book herself.

So when the cold driving rain that comes to Maine's coast for two weeks every fall made the other children restless and eager to be out-of-doors again, Louise was content to rearrange the furniture in all the rooms of the house, then use the treasured crayons her father had bought for her to reproduce them on paper. While the wind rattled the doors and windows and the incessant rain beat down on the roof, inside Louise felt warm and secure as she drew her pictures.

The Rockland Public Library as it appears today.
PHOTOGRAPH BY L. H. BOBER.

Although she was still too young to realize it, she was developing her visual mind. She could remember everything she saw in vivid detail. She couldn't know then the way her life would turn out, but she was beginning to feel the pattern it would take. She had already decided she liked being called an artist. Why she even felt like an artist!

One day, when Louise was nine, she went to the library with her friend Blanche, who liked to read. The library was a beautiful building that had opened just a few years before. It had been built of local granite and was surrounded by tall elm trees. The high curved archways and domed ceiling inside imparted a sense of grandeur to it. The life-size statue of Joan of Arc that Louise loved in the reading room only added to this, and may have made more of an impression on the young Louise than she realized. The statue, made of white plaster, had a soft patina, and Louise admired it whenever she went to the library.

As Blanche was checking out her books the librarian, Nancy Burbank, struck up a conversation. She asked Blanche what she wanted to be when she grew up (a typical adult question).

"A bookkeeper," Blanche answered.

Then she put the same question to Louise.

"I'm going to be an artist," Louise replied. Then, perhaps thinking of the statue, she added quickly, "No, I want to be a sculptor. I don't want color to help me." Then she got so frightened by her unexpected answer that she ran home crying. "How did I know that when I never thought of it before?" she asked.[9]

·T·W·O·

Gathering Treasures

AS THEY grew up the children took on the particular chores each preferred. Nate helped his father in the woods with the lumber. Much of Isaac's land was woodland, and the lumber was milled and stacked during the winter to be used for building in the warm weather. Among the girls, Anita loved to bake and thought that mowing the lawn was fun, Lillian did much of the mending, and Louise helped with the cleaning. She, like her mother, always liked things to be neat and tidy. Also, dusting the furniture gave her the opportunity to move it around. And every week she rearranged the furniture. In fact, she would even peek through the windows of other people's houses on her way back and forth from school and rearrange their furniture in her mind. Even as an adult, living away from the family home for many years, whenever she returned to Rockland to visit, Louise moved the furniture around almost as soon as she arrived.

As Isaac's business prospered he was able to build a

new house for his family next door to the one they were living in on Linden Street. The children were intrigued as they watched the step-by-step process of construction and listened as their father carefully explained some of the intricacies of building and architecture to them. Isaac also explained to them that the Talmud teaches that when you build a house you must always leave a small section unfinished or unpainted in order to remember the destruction of the second Temple in Jerusalem. Louise didn't understand what this meant, but she would never forget it.

Eventually, when the house was completed, and they were ready to move in, Louise was allowed to exercise her passion for arranging furniture. Her mother seems to have recognized her daughter's special gift for spatial arrangements and perhaps even her need to create her immediate environment. She gave her free reign to decide where everything should be placed.

The children's responsibilities at home, coupled with a long school day (opening exercises were at eight forty-five and the last class didn't begin until three o'clock) and the homework that accompanied it, did not allow for much free time. Friday night, though, was always looked forward to eagerly. In the Berliawsky household, as in many Jewish homes, the Sabbath was welcomed each week on Friday evening with the observance of traditional customs and with a special meal.

Isaac would come home from work a little earlier than usual and would find the house shining. Louise had already set the dining-room table with a snowy white cloth and the "good" dishes. At twilight, just as the sun was about to set, the children would watch their mother light and bless the Sabbath candles and then listen to their father sing the *kiddush,* or blessing over the wine. They loved to hear him sing, but they loved even more this chance to drink some wine themselves! Then they would all join in the blessing over the *challah,* the special braided Sabbath bread that Minna and Anita had baked, and the meal would begin. Generally there were fish, soup, chicken and puddings made from noodles or potatoes. The tradition served a dual purpose. It helped to keep alive their Judaism in this alien town, and it brought them together as a family for a brief time each week. A sense of calm seemed to pervade their lives for a few hours and gave them renewed energy for the week to come.

There was another, totally different, reason that Louise looked forward to Friday nights. She and Nate were allowed to go to the movies after dinner. Anita, who wanted to do everything her older sister did, sometimes tagged along. Lillian was too little to accompany them.

On one such evening, when the movie was one that Anita really didn't understand, she curled up in the seat and promptly fell asleep. When it ended, Nate and Louise, still totally absorbed in the story, automatically got up from their seats, left the theater, and walked the mile and a half home, all the while talking about the movie. When they arrived home half an hour later their father, waiting up for them, asked where Anita was. It was only then that they realized that they had completely forgotten about her. Isaac had to walk back across town, awaken the manager, and ask him to unlock the theater door. Anita was still sound asleep in the empty hall.[1]

ONE DAY early in the spring of 1910, when Louise was almost eleven, the children learned that they would have an unexpected day off from school. A newly-built boat was to be launched and, as was the custom when this occurred, the day was declared a holiday in Rockland.

It was particularly exciting because only that past winter all activity in the Rockland Harbor had ceased. The cold was so intense and so prolonged during the winter of 1909 that the water in the harbor had frozen solid.

The children dressed quickly—and with great anticipation—for launching days were always gala events, filled with excitement and fun. Together Nate, Anita and Lillian raced the few blocks from their house to Ingraham Point, near South Street, to the I. L. Snow Shipyard where the launching was to take place. It was one of the few times that they felt a true sense of belonging to this coastal community and took pride in its accomplishments.

At the yard they joined the throngs of people who had come to witness the event, inching their way closer to the shore to get a better look at the beautiful three-masted schooner resting in her wooden cradle. Later they cheered with the crowd as she was christened the *Hugh de Paynes* and then slid gracefully down her "*ways*" and into the water.

But Louise, already far more interested in her art than in anything else, stayed home alone to paint. Other times she would walk along the shore by herself, trying to spot the submarines that came by on trial runs, and listen to the haunting, plaintive sound of the foghorn that often emanated from the lighthouse in Penobscot Bay. The image of the Owl's Head Light, a white conical tower that had been built from birch and locally quarried granite back in 1825, and that sat now atop an evergreen-covered headland at the entrance to Rockland Harbor, was one she would recall with joy more than seventy years later. The water, always so clear and so cold, gave her a feeling of purity and strength.[2]

WHEN LOUISE was ready to start high school she naturally chose art as one of her elective subjects. And there began a relationship with a teacher who would have a profound effect on her life.

Miss Lena F. Cleveland came from nearby Camden and had studied art herself at Pratt Institute in New York. She was a big woman, never married, and with a graciousness and openness about her that appealed to Louise.

When she came to school one day in a purple coat and hat, Louise couldn't resist. She overcame her natural shyness enough to say, "Miss Cleveland, you have a beautiful coat and hat."[3]

Delighted that Louise had noticed, Miss Cleveland explained to her that she had bought the hat because she liked it, *then* searched for a coat to match. Louise was intrigued. Her sense of the unusual in fashion had been sparked. In later years, she also often built an outfit around a beautiful scarf or a piece of jewelry.

In her first term in Miss Cleveland's drawing class Louise had to fight to convince the teacher that the artwork she was bringing to class was her own. Miss Cleveland feared she was tracing it. Once Louise proved to her that the drawings were in fact hers, Miss Cleveland became her staunch supporter and her friend.

She taught Louise her first lessons about light and shade, helped her to understand the use of space, and made her aware of the details of antique furniture. This last would prove invaluable almost forty years later when she began to use fragments of furniture in her sculptures.

Miss Cleveland was a constant source of encouragement. She was convinced that Louise would someday make a name for herself in the art world and frequently told her so. She pushed her to enter art competitions in school. Each time Louise won a competition her self-confidence grew. She became more and more certain that she would be an artist.

She was beginning now, too, to have a sense of her own identity. In an art class one day, when she was completing a watercolor of the living room of a colonial house, a visitor to the classroom was amused to see that the portrait Louise had painted over the mantlepiece was *not*, as was expected, of a typical "colonial" ancestor. Rather, the "ancestor" somehow resembled Louise. Perhaps it was the grandfather she remembered from Russia.

Something else was happening, too. Even though she had been born in a very cold country and had spent the first five years of her life there, she hated the cold, and never got used to the bitter Maine winters. She always felt cold. Somehow, though, she was comfortable in the art room. She was convinced it was warmer there than in any other room in the school. It wasn't until years later that she realized that she had generated her own heat in that room. (Even now, she can warm up on a cold winter day by going into her studio.)

Louise knew she wasn't among the brightest in school. She was an average student and had always been a slow

By the age of seventeen Louise had learned to appreciate—and to reproduce on paper—the beauty of antique furniture. Ink on paper, 1916–1918. SMITHSONIAN INSTITUTION.

reader. Anita was the smart one of the children. In fact, she was skipped a year in school and was graduated with honors. Louise, watching her sister with her head still always in a book, decided that to be a good student you had to read. Since she didn't like to read, but she did love art, she would be an artist—a great one.

But theater was beginning to fascinate her too, and she enjoyed the class on Shakespeare's tragedies. "I could see the walking trees surround Macbeth." *

She took geometry because it was required. But she took it reluctantly. It ". . . didn't make me know myself better. I learned the world, so to speak, totally through art." [4]

When she was elected captain of the high school basketball team she knew that she had been given this dubious honor only because she was the tallest girl in the class. She never became a part of the group, and, in fact, felt the difference between herself and the others keenly. She was always an outsider, never invited to join in the locker room camaraderie or the parties after the games.

One day, standing at her locker after basketball practice, Louise overheard some of the team members talking about the upcoming dance on the following Saturday evening. As they talked about which boy would escort each

* *Macbeth*, Act V, Scene 5
I looked toward Birnam, and . . .
The wood began to move.

The girls in Louise's high school class wore middy blouses to school for special events. Louise Berliawsky—fifth from left. SMITHSONIAN INSTITUTION.

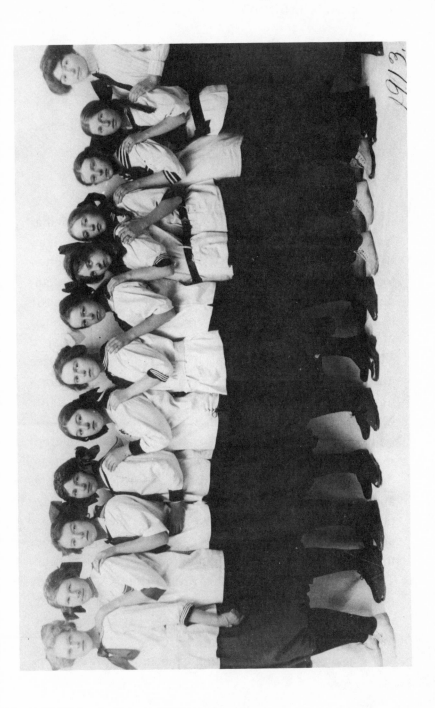

1913.

girl, Louise heard the captain of the boys' team say, "Do I have to take that Jew?"

The pain was sharp and deep.

But as the Rockland teenagers shut them out of their social milieu, the bond among the four Berliawsky children grew even stronger.[5]

AS THEY grew older, all the children, the girls as well as Nate, were taught by their father to understand the construction of a house—and to judge its quality. Isaac often took Louise and Anita to look at a house he was contemplating buying and asked them to appraise it. They quickly learned to evaluate real estate and were generally right. At the same time, the squared-off rooms in the box-shaped colonial houses that were typical of that time and that place were unconsciously impressing themselves on Louise's mind, as was the overwhelming presence of the trees in the Maine landscape.

Both Isaac and Minna believed that their children, regardless of sex, should be educated. They were aware that they had come to a new world filled with opportunity, and they wanted their children to be able to take advantage of this. They recognized Louise's artistic talent very early and encouraged her to pursue it. They never allowed her to feel that being female would in any way be a handicap. To them, it was ability that was important. As did many immigrant families at that time, they yearned for "the best" for their children—the best clothes, the best food, the best education.

Isaac worked hard and long to accomplish these goals.

The streetcar at that time cost only five cents, but Isaac walked to and from work. He could walk faster. And often he didn't eat dinner until after his family had finished.

He was a high-strung, ambitious man, but sensitive and caring as well. He expected much of his children and sometimes lost his temper when they weren't quick to respond. Louise, although occasionally fearful of this, nonetheless looked up to him and took her strength from him.

But he was gentle with Minna and tried hard to please her, although she was never able to accept comfort and love from him. The children learned early to ask for her permission for something. They knew that if their mother said "yes," their father would not disagree.

Minna was always understanding and supportive of her children. While she never adjusted to Rockland, as her husband did, and was never happy there, she did maintain her sense of humor. Louise adored her.

Isaac's love of music inspired his three daughters to study voice and piano. Anita studied the violin, also. When the phonograph was perfected, Isaac was one of the first people in Rockland to buy one. Then he built up a large collection of records. Eventually, he owned all the recordings of the great Italian singer, Enrico Caruso. At that time Caruso was at the height of his career as the leading tenor at the Metropolitan Opera House in New York. He typified all that was colorful and dramatic in opera, and the family loved to listen to him. Music filled the house.[6]

One day, as Louise rounded the corner onto Linden Street on her way home from school, she was surprised to see a huge truck parked in front of her house. Her heart began to pound. What new gift had her father bought for them? She was soon joined by her brother and sisters, and

they watched wide-eyed as the delivery men carefully un-
loaded a shiny black piano from the truck and carried it up
the stairs and into their house. Excitement ran high in the
Berliawsky house that night.

After that Louise would often sing to her sisters' ac-
companiment, but, as much as he loved it, Isaac rarely
found time to sit and listen. He was too high keyed and
energetic to be able to simply sit. Years later Louise would
comment, "When he came home . . . it was like an engine
. . . going chuga-chuga-chug."[7]

Still, Isaac's sensitivity to art, his respect for cultural
life, was passed on to his eldest daughter. It was she who
was the moving force behind any family cultural project. It
was she who was constantly urging her brother and sisters
to participate in cultural activities in Rockland.

Isaac loved to collect antiques, and he communicated
this impulse to collect to Louise also. His birthday and
holiday gifts to his children were frequently antiques, and
he had to build a separate storehouse to hold his own collection, for Minna allowed only "new" furniture in their
home.[8] As Isaac was filling a warehouse with his collection
of antique furniture and toys, Louise was busy gathering
pebbles, marbles, bits of fabric and old lace, trinkets, pieces
of driftwood—anything her discerning eye spotted—then
putting them into boxes and stacking them on the floor or
if she could, hanging them on the walls in her room. When
Lillian teased her, suggesting that soon she'd have to move
out to make room for the boxes, Louise simply ignored her.

Minna, who by now had asked her family to call her
by the more American name of Ann, was not as apprecia-
tive of art as her husband. She was, nonetheless, a bright
and beautiful woman with a flair for fashion. In her own
way she made fashion an art.

She had exquisite taste in clothes. She bought only the finest and most expensive dresses and hats, then took meticulous care of them and kept them in perfect condition for years.[9]

Since the life of Rockland's almost exclusively Gentile community centered around the church, Minna had few friends and rarely went out. At that time, the few other Jewish families of Rockland all lived on the north side of town. The Berliawsky house was on the south side, and the distance between was far too great for a casual visit.

Sunday was the one day Isaac spent with his family. He liked to stroll with them through downtown Rockland. They were a striking group, and he was extremely proud of them.

Minna, who never realized how naturally beautiful she was, would rouge her cheeks (an Old World custom, but somewhat scandalous in Rockland, Maine) and spend several hours dressing. The result was always lovely, and Isaac loved to show her off. But, while he enjoyed the admiring glances of his many friends and acquaintances, Minna, who was terribly shy, hated it. She was always embarrassed by them. She would hold her head high, trying hard to hide behind a bold front. Louise imitated this carriage and thought, "Someday it will be my turn to be the star."

Minna's concern with clothes helped Louise to develop her own sense of style. She loved to wear hats and often made unusual ones for herself. Once, when she was fourteen, she painted butterflies on a piece of linen, folded the fabric into pleats, and attached it to a hat frame. Then she wore the hat to school every day.[10] This passion for hats would carry over into her adult life. Years later Louise would become known in the art world as "The Hat." She loved, also, the look and the dress of the Pemaquid Indians who lived on nearby reservations and frequently came into town. Their appearance was fascinating to her, and she began to imitate it. She learned to appreciate their art and often browsed in the local antique shops, learning all she could about American Indian art.

Louise used her flair for fashion for her sisters' benefit too. Anita, particularly, loved to "dress up." Then Louise would simply wrap something around her, add a scarf or a belt, and suddenly, there was an outfit.

On the other hand, their mother's insistence that her girls wear beautiful and expensive dresses to school made them feel different from the other children. Louise felt this difference most keenly. She, of all the Berliawsky children, had the sharpest memories of Russia and, consequently, always felt like a stranger in Rockland.[11] Her unusual beauty, her exotic clothes, her fluency in two strange languages, Yiddish and Russian, her already visible artistic talent (she sang, she played the piano, she drew beautiful pictures), added to her shyness all seemed to set her apart from her classmates and to add to her growing sense of isolation and loneliness. So she, like her mother, hid behind a proud bearing and retreated more and more into herself and her art. The pattern of her life was becoming more sharply defined.

Trapped in the "Promised Land"

IT WAS when Louise was seventeen and a half years old and a senior in high school that Rockland's shipbuilding industry had an impact on her personal life. That spring of 1917 the United States was engaged in World War I, and Rockland, Maine, had become a strategic area. Many of the United States Navy's damaged ships docked there for repairs.

Louise, fulfilling a requirement for graduation for students following the commercial course of study, was working in downtown Rockland for part of the term. She was employed as secretary to Arthur Littlefield of the Littlefield law firm, whose clients included several shipping companies.

One day a handsome gentleman walked into her office, announced that he was Bernard Nevelson, and that he had come to pick up some documents pertaining to his shipping business that the firm had prepared for him. Impulsively, Louise answered him in Yiddish.

Captivated by this bold and beautiful young woman, he sat down to talk to her. He told her that he and his three younger brothers had been born in Russia, that their father had owned "woods" there, and that now he was from New York. He and his family were in the shipping business on Wall Street. Their firm supplied ships to the United States Navy. His casual references to President Woodrow Wilson made Louise feel that the Nevelsons were on friendly terms with the president of the United States.

Louise, intrigued by this man, by the wealth and power that seemed to surround him, and by their common heritage, invited him home for dinner.

A few days later Bernard reciprocated by inviting Louise to have dinner with him at the Thorndike Hotel, where he was staying. Louise was nervous, but curious. She had never had dinner in a hotel before, and she wondered what it would be like.

She dressed carefully that evening, hoping that her pounding heart didn't show. Although she wouldn't admit it, she was grateful when her brother Nate, always protective of his sisters, insisted that he would walk her to the hotel.

When she arrived, she was not prepared for the big French sea captain with his great beard who accompanied Bernard. She had never seen anyone like him. All through dinner she had to work hard to concentrate on what Bernard was saying to her. She was casting surreptitious glances at the captain, fantasizing that he was about to whisk her away on his ship.

Louise's high school graduation picture portrays a beautiful young woman (1917). PHOTOGRAPH COURTESY OF ANITA WEINSTEIN.

She did learn that Bernard was in his late forties and married to a young woman who was about to give birth to their first child. So when Bernard returned to New York and wrote to her, Louise was afraid to answer. Then, that summer, shortly after Louise had graduated from high school, a letter arrived from Bernard saying that his youngest brother, Charles, was coming to Rockland to see about their ships.

A few days later Charles did arrive and telephoned Louise. She talked to him for a while, then accepted his invitation to have dinner with him that evening. It would be her first real date. When she put the receiver back on its hook she thought for a few minutes about some things Bernard had said in his letters, and guessed that he had encouraged Charles to come to Rockland to see her. Then she found her mother and confided to her that she had the feeling that Charles Nevelson would propose marriage to her that evening—and that she would accept.

Her mother was confused. She knew that Louise planned to attend Pratt Art Institute in New York in September. And she had heard her say many times that she would never marry. But in her quiet way Minna simply warned her daughter that combining her art and marriage would be difficult. Then she said no more.

And that evening Charles Nevelson did propose to Louise Berliawsky. When she explained to him that she had just graduated from high school and expected to study art that fall, he seemed agreeable. Why couldn't she marry and still pursue her studies, he asked. At that time it was not unusual for two people to enter into a marriage for practical rather than romantic reasons. Often families arranged these matches.

Charles was fifteen years older than Louise and much shorter than she, but he was an educated and wealthy gentleman from New York. He offered her a chance to leave Rockland, to study art, and perhaps even to live in a large and luxurious home in the middle of New York City. He offered her protection, comfort, security. He agreed that they would not have children. And her parents liked him. She seemed on the threshold of achieving her goal.

So Louise Berliawsky of Rockland, Maine, found herself with a one-carat diamond solitaire on her finger, engaged to be married to Charles Nevelson of New York. But she felt little of the excitement and anticipation that generally surrounds a bride-to-be. She even confided to Anita that she really didn't like her ring—it was too conventional for her.

———————

EXCITEMENT did come in no small measure, though, a short time later when Charles invited Louise and Minna to come to New York to meet his family. This is what she had been dreaming of—waiting for. This had been her father's dream, too, for as long as she could remember. How often he had talked of moving his family there! New York, the city of high fashion, of skyscrapers, of mansions, of grandeur and riches—theater capital of the world, home of the arts—this is what she craved, and soon she would be part of it.

Mother and daughter traveled to New York by train. They stayed at the Martha Washington Hotel on East Twenty-ninth Street, one of the first hotels in New York

City that was exclusively for women. And they saw the city.

They saw the tall buildings that Louise loved. Her favorite was the Flatiron Building, so named because it resembled the flatirons people used then to press their clothes. Designed to conform to the triangular piece of land on which it was built (the scissor-like intersection where Broadway and Fifth Avenue converge at Twenty-third Street), the building narrowed down to a rounded point on the north end, almost like a slice of pie. Completed in 1902, it was the first steel skyscraper erected in New York. Contemporary critics praised it as a marvel of engineering, but they condemned its unusual design as an architectural monstrosity, a "vast horror." Louise loved it. Perhaps it was just this unconventional appearance that appealed to her even then. Today the building is a designated landmark.

And Louise loved the mansions—the great nineteenth-century houses that lined Fifth Avenue then. Often, when Charles was working, Louise and Minna would stroll up Fifth Avenue's broad sidewalks to where Central Park began, admiring the magnificent private houses along the way. The lower part of the Avenue, from Thirty-fourth to Thirty-ninth Streets, was just becoming the country's leading fashion center as stores such as the beautiful Lord & Taylor were opening their doors. Minna spent money with abandon there as she added the latest New York fashions to her daughter's rapidly growing trousseau. What great fun they had together, indulging their shared passion for clothes!

One day, Charles took them downtown to Wall Street, the financial heart of the nation, to show them his offices. The Nevelsons had two companies: Nevelson Brothers

Shipping at 42 Broadway; and Polish American Navigation Company at 120 Broadway. From there, as they looked down Broadway, they could see Battery Park, the liners and tugs in New York Harbor, and the Statue of Liberty standing sentinel in the distance.

They lunched at the exclusive Century Club. In the evening they dined and danced at the roof garden of the elegant St. Regis Hotel. Louise loved the riches, the opulence, the grandeur that was New York. Her only complaint was that the pace of the city wasn't fast enough!

She was more certain than ever that New York was where she wanted to live. She knew she had made the right choice. She was sure, even then, that New York would become her "Promised Land."

AFTER SUNDOWN on the warm, cloudy evening of Saturday, June 12, 1920, Charles and Louise were married at the Copley Plaza Hotel in Boston. Rabbi Harry Levy of Temple Israel in Boston officiated. It was a small wedding, with members of the Nevelson family coming from New York, and the Berliawskys coming from Maine. Only Nate could not attend. He was serving with the Army in World War I.

The newlyweds honeymooned in New Orleans, where the Nevelsons owned ships. Then, after a brief stay in New York, they took a second trip to Cuba. Charles conducted business there as well.

And so began for Louise what promised to be a life of wealth and ease—the life of a New York society matron.

WHEN Louise settled in New York after her marriage she was still very shy. She found it far more difficult than she had anticipated to mingle in the social milieu of her husband's family and friends. The leisurely life of upper-middle-class society repulsed her. She could not be one of the ladies who played bridge or mah-jong in the afternoons or served tea to one another following an afternoon of shopping. She had to pursue her art.

So she began voice lessons with Metropolitan Opera coach Estelle Liebling and enrolled in dramatics classes. She also studied painting for a brief period with painter and art historian Theresa Bernstein. She visited museums and art galleries. She attended dance recitals. She reached out to all the arts. And Charles was happy to pay for this. She no longer felt the need to attend Pratt Art Institute, as her art teachers in Rockland had. She was in a position now to have private lessons.

New York in the twenties was an exciting city. It was the undisputed capital of the theater. In one season alone —1921—a galaxy of performers perhaps unequaled in history appeared on Broadway. Katharine Cornell, Eva Le-Gallienne, Lionel, Ethel and John Barrymore, Alfred Lunt and Lynn Fontanne, Helen Hayes, Tallulah Bankhead, Al Jolson, Fred and Adele Astaire, John Drew and Otis Skinner were only *some* of the greats who played that year.[1] Louise saw many of them.

And she was in the packed house that attended a concert by Sergei Rachmaninoff at Carnegie Hall shortly after he had arrived in the United States. This great piano virtuoso and composer had just escaped from Russia. She watched as the tall, gaunt Russian strode across the stage, sat at the piano, adjusted his coat-tails and, with the impressive concentration that always marked his playing, interpreted the music of Chopin, Liszt and Tschaikowsky.

Louise sat spellbound as the rafters rang with applause for this popular Russian pianist, and she lingered until the last minute as he played encore after encore.

Louise was trying to absorb all that New York had to offer. She understood that all the arts were one. To comprehend them all was essential. "One supported the other," she felt. She knew she had to "delve into life." And art was life to her.

THEN, in 1922, on February 23, her freedom to pursue the arts suddenly came to a halt. She gave birth to a son, whom they named Myron. While she loved "Mike" dearly, her sense of the immense responsibility of a child was overwhelming. The thought that she had brought another human being into the world, and that she must now care for him was more than she could deal with. She simply wasn't ready for motherhood. This, coupled with the loss of her freedom and the realization that she was no longer in control, sent her into a state of deep depression. Neither her mother's frequent visits to help her, nor the fact that her sisters alternated between living with her and living nearby helped to ease the burden for her. Nor did Charles's obvious delight in his newborn son, and his willingness to provide his wife with any material comforts she might want, help to ease the situation.

She knew that emotionally she and Charles were growing further and further apart. She recognized now that there had never been the real love or common interests on which to build a marriage. She felt trapped.

·F·O·U·R·

Search for an Anchor

WHEN MIKE was two years old Charles bought a "mansion" in Mt. Vernon, and moved his family there. Louise would have loved a house in New York, but Charles said no. He wanted Mike to grow up "in the country." Soon Anita came to stay with them. She offered her sister help with her baby, companionship and moral support. When they could, the two women drove the Peerless car to New York and gradually began, once again, to attend concerts, museums, and the theater.

Then, at Anita's urging, Louise registered for Saturday afternoon classes at the Art Students League, and, two years later, took a brief series of private painting lessons.

It was at this time that the International Theatre Exposition was being held at Steinway Hall, in New York. One cold, blustering day just after it was opened on February 27, 1926, Louise went to see it. She was so taken with the exhibit that she took Lillian, who had recently come to New York, and Anita back to see it with her again and again. The exhibit, organized by Friederich Kiesler, an Austrian set designer who had just come to the United States, included some of the most avant-garde examples of set design at that time. Included among the works being shown were several by Pablo Picasso.* In the program for the exhibition Kiesler set forth his ideas for the ideal stage: "The contemporary theatre calls for the vitality of life itself . . . it demands . . . space in the truest sense of the word."[1] This first awareness of the world of the theater, and her first view of a work by Picasso would be indelibly etched on her mind.

That summer Louise took Mike back to Maine for a brief vacation. While she was there she enrolled in an art program in Boothbay Harbor. When she had been there just a short while, the director told her he'd be happy to refund her tuition. He felt she wasn't ready for his school. "No," she said, "I'll stay." And a few weeks later the director selected her painting as "the most vital because it was so dynamic and colorful." Years later, commenting on this, Louise said, "Now, had I left when he suggested, I would have felt so defeated. But I stayed. I never ran."[2]

IN THE early 1920s, when Charles and Louise were first married, New York was the financial capital of the world— and Wall Street was the center of the world's money. New York banks established branches around the globe, and money poured into Wall Street from all over. As the twen-

---

* In 1917, Picasso had spent a great deal of time creating stage designs for the Ballets Russes.

ties progressed, though, cracks in the system began to appear. While the stock market didn't actually crash until October of 1929, by 1927, the Nevelsons were beginning to feel the effects of the economic depression.

Gradually diminishing finances finally forced them to sell the house in Mt. Vernon and move to Brooklyn. Again Louise begged Charles to buy a house in Manhattan. Again, he refused. Lillian moved into the Brooklyn house with them, and Anita, who had married, moved with her husband into an apartment nearby.

During the year before they moved, the International Theatre Exposition had frequently occupied Louise's thoughts. In fact, the exhibit had had such a profound effect on her that soon after they moved to Brooklyn she enrolled in the Theatre Arts Institute, a school organized by Friederich Kiesler and Princess Norina Matchabelli. Lillian took care of Mike. She was also his kindergarten teacher in a private school near their home in Brooklyn in 1927–28.

Kiesler and Princess Matchabelli had worked together in Max Reinhardt's theater in Berlin, where Kiesler had designed the stage setting, and Matchabelli had been the star. They had recently come to New York with him. Louise thought Norina Matchabelli was one of the most beautiful women she had ever seen. She was intrigued by that lady's sense of fashion. Soon she found herself wearing the big hats she used to love when she was a teenager in Rockland—perhaps imitating Norina's penchant for wide-brimmed hats.

Max Reinhardt, whose achievements in theater were legend, possessed such a broad and comprehensive knowledge of the theater and strong personal magnetism that he was able to inspire to greatness all who worked with him. It was his belief that drama was the most direct art—since people rather than stone, or wood, or canvas are its medium of expression.[3]

The school, set up in a brownstone in Brooklyn, was actually a laboratory for the contemporary stage, and exposed Louise to some of Max Reinhardt's views. It served, also, to help her to recognize the close relationship between art and the theater. She began to move toward a greater interest in theater and in voice, and away from painting. She and Lillian began to take singing lessons again—as they had when they were children.

But Charles was becoming jealous of the increasing amount of time Louise was spending away from home. He set rigid standards for her and insisted that she comply with them. He was a kind and generous man, particularly with their son. And though he enjoyed letting the little boy use his razor to whittle small animals out of wood, he seemed to resent his wife's artistic talent and objected to her interests conflicting with what he considered to be her duties as a wife and mother. Louise, attempting to explain this years later, said that in her husband's circle ". . . you could know Beethoven, but God forbid if you *were* Beethoven."[4] As he continued to discourage all her attempts to pursue a creative career, Louise began to feel that he was choking her. She had had complete freedom as she was growing up and she had always seen her father cater to her mother, so she found it impossible to understand Charles's actions. Nor could she acquiesce to his demands. She could not—or would not—accept the responsibility of marriage.

Perhaps her inability—or unwillingness—to compromise stemmed from her need to be completely free. "I needed . . . total time for myself," she has said.

When Charles told her he expected her home by

seven-thirty to have dinner with him, Louise retorted, "What do we have a maid for if not to get your dinner?"

It probably never occurred to her that Charles might have wanted her home for dinner simply because he enjoyed being with her. He wanted a wife. She wanted art.

BY 1929, the Nevelsons' financial situation had deteriorated even more, and they were forced to move from the Brooklyn house to an apartment on East Ninety-first Street in Manhattan. (Anita took an apartment on East Eighty-ninth Street). Louise gave up her studies at the Theatre Arts Institute and took Mike out of private school.

She entered into another period of depression. The many moves, the upheaval, the cessation of her studies, the uncertainty of where her life was going, became more than she could cope with. She was overcome by a feeling of lethargy. She seemed to be functioning mechanically— almost as if she were in a trance. Life had little meaning for her.

Then, one day, when Mike was in school, she took a walk to the Metropolitan Museum of Art on Fifth Avenue at Eighty-second Street—not too far from where they were living. There was an exhibition there of Noh robes—the elaborately styled kimonos worn by the actors in the classical drama of Japan. These were finely woven of sheer gold cloth with medallions of gold superimposed. Louise had never seen anything so delicate, so exquisite. "It was the reverse of what people think, that gold material was a little vulgar . . . It was the height of human refinement."[5]

She sat down right there and cried as she had never

cried before. The impact of the beauty of this exhibit struck a chord deep within her—that seemed to open her up, to bring her back to life.

She began once again to frequent museums and art galleries. The Museum of Modern Art was being formed then and she went there often. There she saw the first Picasso paintings that had come from Europe and the paintings of Matisse. Picasso, she has said, gave her "a definition of structure of the world and every object in the world." A few months later she enrolled again in morning classes at the Art Students League.

Her first teacher there was Kenneth Hayes Miller. Miller emphasized the intuitive approach to art and urged his students to find their own artistic selves. He communicated to his students his belief that painting came before their personal lives and reinforced Louise's commitment to art as a way of life.

His interest in the sculptural qualities of painting, "his urging to 'reach around' the object," may have been a factor in Louise's later decision to sculpt. For while she had impulsively stated when she was nine years old that she would be a sculptor when she grew up, her interest at this point in her life seemed to encompass all the arts. She had not yet determined what specific aspect of art she would pursue.[6]

Perhaps unwittingly, Miller, by his encouragement of Louise's work, was playing the same role that Miss Cleveland had played so many years before. Surrounded by other young people who were dedicated to art—seeing them work and sharing ideas with them—gave Louise a feeling of comfort and strength, a sense of *belonging*. She was slowly regaining her self-confidence.[7]

Soon she began to attend afternoon classes with Kimon Nicolaides as well. It was in his class that she first learned of the artist Hans Hofmann, the only person in the world, she was told, who could teach her to understand cubism and the works of Picasso and Matisse.

Hofmann had founded the Schule für Moderne Kunst in 1915 in Schwabing, the artists' district of Munich, in Germany. Over the years his reputation had grown, and increasing numbers of American artists were traveling to Munich to study with him. His enthusiasm, his personal aura, made the world of art seem both exciting and important to his students. Louise began to feel that she, too, must attend his school.

By now it was 1931, and Louise had been married to Charles for eleven years. But the marriage had steadily deteriorated. She now felt that she could no longer continue to live with him. She took Mike to Rockland to visit her family and to try to sort out her thoughts.

Minna understood her daughter's dilemma and could empathize with her. In a quiet conversation one evening she told her, "You don't have to stay married. Before that you were so vital."[8] She, who had never been happy in her own marriage, recognized that her daughter needed her freedom to survive. In fact, it may well have been Minna's example of unhappiness in marriage that made it impossible for Louise to build a successful one herself. Now Minna urged Louise to leave Mike in Rockland and go to Munich to study.

One of Louise's stark, linear drawings of the 1930s, reminiscent of Henri Matisse. Note that the head, feet and hands were omitted for the sake of composition. **Leaning Nude Figure,** *c. 1930, pencil on paper.* COLBY COLLEGE ART MUSEUM.

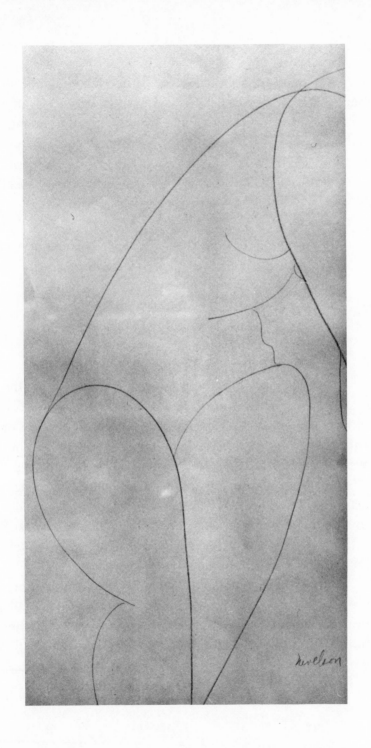

While the economic depression had taken its toll on Isaac's finances as well as Charles's, her brother Nate's hotel business was thriving and he was happy to finance the trip.

Louise, though, worried about leaving because she knew that her mother was ill and was facing the prospect of surgery. Minna's response was typical of her:

> "Louise, you must go. You always wanted to continue in your art. If I don't survive, it will make no difference. If I live, I'll see you when you get back. You go and study. We'll send you an allowance, and we'll take care of Mike and see that he has everything he needs."

With her mother's quiet strength providing Louise the courage she needed, she separated from Charles, left Mike in Rockland, and sailed for Germany late in the winter of 1931. She was physically and emotionally exhausted, but she knew she was taking an important and necessary step.

Uncertain about permanently dissolving her marriage, fearful of relinquishing the security her life as a New York society matron afforded her, and, above all else, wracked with guilt at leaving Mike, she was struggling desperately for a reality, "something to give me an anchor."[9]

Years later she would say, "the guilts of motherhood were the worst guilts in the world for me. They were really insurmountable. You see, you are depriving another human being of so many things . . . that's the price, the great price."[10]

·F·I·V·E·

Dance to Freedom

AT HOFMANN'S SCHOOL in Munich Louise attended daily drawing classes. The instruction was primarily in life drawing in charcoal. But Hofmann stressed the mysterious process of creation itself, the intuitive aspect of art, as Miller had in his classes at the Art Students League. And Hofmann taught his famous "push and pull" theory. He demonstrated that shadow was as valid as light. "We wouldn't see light without shadow. We wouldn't see shadow without light." Louise learned that "Cubism gives you a *block* of space for light, a *block* of space for shadow." She was learning to understand the cube. "When I went to Hofmann in 1931 in Germany, I recognized it, I identified it, and it gave me the key to my stability."[1] Fifty years later her work would still have the stamp of the Cubist movement.

In spite of what she learned, though, Louise was bitterly disappointed. It was at this time that Adolf Hitler was rising to power in Germany, and the political climate there was becoming stifling for many members of the art community. As a Jew, Hans Hofmann knew he had to leave and began channeling his energy into making the necessary arrangements to get out of Germany. He taught only one class a week. The remaining classes were supervised by his assistant. Hofmann's legendary enthusiasm for teaching began to wane, and his interest in his students narrowed to the few who could help him accomplish his goal. Louise was not among them. In fact, in a final blow to her self-esteem, Hofmann told her she would never be an artist and asked her to leave his class. She was shattered. Then, just a few months later, Nazi political power forced Hofmann to close his school.

THE ONE bright spot in her life then was the mail she received from nine-year-old Mike. When she sent him a little gift from Germany, he thanked her but told her not to send any more. He advised her to save her money and buy paints instead ". . . 'cause times are hard and you shouldn't spend it when you need it for paints. Nathan will send some money soon."[2] Another time, when she had sent him a picture of herself, he wrote,

> I recived [sic] your photograph
> Grandma thinks you look crazy,
> but she's old and don't know
> much I think you look good
> just like a great artist.[3]

That spring he wrote:

I am getting along fine in
sckool [sic]
The kids call me the New York monkey
but I don't care a [sic] *call them the Maine*
Maineacks. . . .
How are you getting along in sckool, [sic]
do the cridicks [sic] *like you. I*
hope you are studing. [sic][4]

While she was in Munich Louise spent many evenings
in the cafés and cabarets with other young artists and students. They would sit around all evening, talking and singing. They discussed politics, they discussed art—and they
sang American songs. Prewar Munich was much taken
with American jazz and popular music. Louise, tall, graceful, strikingly beautiful, who knew all the songs and loved
to sing, suddenly found herself the center of attraction.

As her singing and acting talents were recognized, her
self-confidence gradually began to return. Then, when
some friends who were involved in theater there offered
her a bit part in a movie, her old interest in the theater was
rekindled. Seeing this as a means of earning enough money
to pay for her passage back home, she accepted.

And she was ready to go home. She had just received
a poem from Mike begging her to return, telling her how
much he missed her after just a few short months:

February is drawing near
The nights are cold but clear
But a present will not bring me cheer
All I want is to see you dear[5]

After playing several parts in Munich she accepted a friend's invitation to work in films in Vienna, Austria. But she was happy there for a brief time only. Her work as an actress in several minor roles left her restless and unsatisfied. While she enjoyed the acting itself, she resented the wasted time spent waiting for directions. No doubt her energetic spirit would have preferred being the director! What she did love though were the other elements of moviemaking—the cameras, the lights, the sets.

STILL ADRIFT, not knowing which course to follow, her priorities not yet sorted out and her problems still unresolved, Louise decided to leave Vienna in April. She knew she was not far from Salzburg, and she wanted to see it. She had heard tell of the beautiful architecture in this Austrian city. She knew that Mozart had been born in Salzburg, and that Max Reinhardt, who had also lived there, was one of the originators and principal producers of its annual music and dance festival. When she found that it was easy to get there by train, she decided to go.

Salzburg is snuggled in the foothills of the Alps, and Louise loved it immediately. It was snowing when she arrived, and the city was blanketed in white. One day, as she walked through a mountain pass all alone, she suddenly found herself singing—in a voice that seemed to want to reach the top of the mountain. "The geography of the land contained sound," she explained it later. "[It] was a landscape that demanded sound and echo."[6]

From Salzburg, Louise traveled through Italy on her

way to Paris. Then, in Paris, she spent her days soaking up all she could of the work of the masters in the Louvre Museum. She took time, also, to visit the Musée de L'Homme, the museum of African sculpture. The masks and the full figures excited her. She had never seen anything like it before. She was particularly moved by a carved African figure of a leopard. As she stood and gazed at it, she sensed the power—not of the animal, but of its forms. She was caught up in the power and the energy of African sculpture.

But she was still depressed, confused about what to do with her life, and terribly lonely. She finally decided to go home.

Louise returned to New York and went to Rockland to see Mike and her family. When she found Mike happy and well cared for and her mother fully recovered, she went on to New York, where she settled in a loft by herself to draw, paint, and sculpt. Her marriage was ended.*

Louise lived this way for the next nine months. But soon she began to feel the need to seriously study the work of the great European masters. Then riding on the subway in Manhattan one day, the black iron stanchions evoked memories of the African sculpture she had seen at Musée de L'Homme. Her initial exposure to the art treasures of Paris had served only to whet her appetite for more. So, with her mother's encouragement once again, she pawned the diamond bracelet that Charles had given her when Mike was born and used the money to book passage on the *France*. In Paris she renewed her independent study of the artists.

* She was legally divorced ten years later.

Her objective was to see the art, and this she did. She visited the museums, the cathedrals, the Palace of Versailles. She was excited anew by the work of Picasso that she saw: "Picasso has a Spanish fire and restlessness . . . French art is too cultivated. . . ." But she was too shy to attempt to meet him.

Still desperately lonely, but with an understanding now of the wide difference between European and American art, she recognized that she ". . . could be a leaf on the tree in Paris, but I could be that tree in America."[7] Fall of 1932 found her back in New York. She had remained in Paris only six weeks.

WHEN SHE RETURNED she learned that Hans Hofmann was teaching at the Art Students League. Hofmann had established himself in New York and was regaining his old enthusiasm for teaching. Soon he would be known as "the sparkplug of the New York school."

Still brooding over his rejection of her work in Munich, Louise nonetheless found the courage to go back to his class in New York. And Hofmann redeemed himself in her eyes. He praised one of her drawings in front of the class one day, calling it "bigger than life."[8] Once again, as in the art class in Boothbay Harbor a few years before, her devotion to her art—and her determination to succeed— paid off. She knew she was a good draftsman with a sharp eye and a free hand. Although she was often "bottled up" inside, she always felt free to let her hand go. She never stopped to measure. She knew what was right—and she loved the movement.

Suddenly, too, she found that she had friends. Many of the students in her art classes were, like herself, immigrants. At that time there was a large influx of artists to the United States. They were able to accept Louise on her own terms.

One of the students in the class was Marjorie Eaton, a young woman from a wealthy California family. Marjorie, like Louise, was interested in *all* the arts. While she later became very involved with the theater, at that time she was particularly interested in painting and had recently spent five years living and painting on an Indian reservation in Taos, New Mexico.

Marjorie watched Louise for a week, and, intrigued by her beauty and by her intense devotion to art, finally spoke to her. "I was impressed by her [Louise's] independence, and by her ability to remove herself from a destructive situation," Marjorie would say later. Louise invited Marjorie to tea, and the two became fast friends.[9]

Through Marjorie, Louise met Diego Rivera, a pioneer Mexican mural painter who, with his wife Frida Kahlo, had recently come to New York from Mexico. Marjorie had known Diego and Frida in Mexico some years before. Louise was intrigued by Frida—petite and strikingly beautiful in her Mexican outfits and Mexican jewelry —and a fine painter also. Frida had been severely injured in a bus accident when she was eighteen and remained permanently crippled. She had begun to paint as therapy.

Diego Rivera had worked in Paris from 1911 to 1921, years that saw the birth of Cubism, and he knew many of the artists associated with that movement. While he was in Europe he had traveled to Italy where he absorbed the lessons of the muralists of the Italian Renaissance. When he returned to his native Mexico in the late twenties, he combined Mexican folk art with Italian fresco * techniques. His love for things Indian, and his use of pre-Columbian ** forms in his painting, did much to awaken Mexicans to their past. When his fame spread to the United States the Rockefeller family invited him to come to New York to paint a mural for Rockefeller Center. It was this that he was working on then.

When Marjorie showed some of Louise's drawings to Diego, he asked Louise to become one of his assistants, along with the artist Ben Shahn, on a smaller mural he was doing called *The Workers*. At first, Louise was delighted. She did historical research for him. She mixed paint and applied washes. She copied small sketches onto the large mural.[10]

She became friendly with Frida, whose fiercely independent spirit appealed to her, and with Ben Shahn, a painter who had recently attracted attention by a series of gouaches† on social issues. He and Louise became good friends. And Louise met other painters, sculptors, writers, dancers, musicians and diplomats who were Diego's friends.

When an empty loft became available in the building on West Thirteenth Street where Diego and Frida lived and worked, Louise and Marjorie decided to pool their resources and rent it together. Now Louise was spending most of her time with the Riveras and their friends.

* a painting executed on plaster.
** pre-Columbian art—art before Christopher Columbus arrived in the Americas.
† opaque watercolor paint

DIEGO WAS an outgoing, friendly and generous man completely devoted to his art. He was always surrounded by a group of admiring artists and friends. Often, after a long and tiring day of painting, they would all go out to dinner together. Their favorite haunt was a little Italian restaurant in the cellar of a building on Fourteenth Street. There, in the course of the evening, they would use powdered sugar, drops of wine, pepper, whatever was available, to compose a "painting" on the white tablecloth. They would move around the table, each person taking a turn, until, at the end of the evening, the tablecloth had become a landscape. ". . . we had a gay time. We used to carry on."[11]

In the meantime Lillian had married Ben Mildwoff, a young artist in New York, and their home became another meeting place for Louise's friends.

Louise was beginning to relax. She was learning the joys of friendship, she was living in New York independent of Charles, and Mike was happy with his grandparents in Maine. She was becoming a part of the group of struggling young artists in New York.

While Louise was enjoying this newfound independence and her association with Diego Rivera, at the same time she began to feel that the work she was doing for him was stifling her own creativity. Nor did Diego's fresco technique appeal to her. She knew that she "had to seek [her] own way of communicating."[12] She admired Diego as a person, but his political leanings troubled her. (Rivera was a member of the Communist Party in Mexico.) She wanted no part of his social protest paintings.

Then the Rockefellers discovered that Rivera had painted the head of Lenin, the Russian Communist leader, into the mural they had commissioned for Rockefeller Center. They were outraged. They stopped him from completing the work, paid him the five thousand dollars he had been promised, and covered the wall with plain canvas. Eventually, the mural was destroyed.

But Louise recognized that she had gained much from Diego. She had learned to work on a large scale. Her interest in Indian art had been reawakened, and she was more certain than ever that art would be her life.

ONE OF THE ARTISTS who came to watch Diego paint was the sculptor John Flanagan. His wife was studying dance with a young woman named Ellen Kearns. One evening the Flanagans brought Ellen along with them to dinner, and Ellen very quickly asked Louise to join her dance class.

This was just what Louise needed as an outlet for her own creativity. She began to study with Ellen. Conveniently, Ellen's studio was in the same building.

Louise had always felt that a body discipline was necessary. She had studied voice as a child, and then again as a young woman just after her marriage. Then, when Martha Graham moved to Tenth Street while Louise was living on Thirteenth, Louise would often see her walking in the neighborhood, and her interest in dance was awakened. She had watched Martha Graham and had been captivated by the woman and by her dancing.[13]

Graham was a pioneer in the field of dance. She was

developing a new vision of dance—with freedom to express oneself. She would eventually be called "the greatest dance celebrity in the United States,"[14] and Louise would say of her years later, "Graham was . . . movement of the twentieth century."[15]

Ellen's dancing was very much like Martha Graham's. She invented her technique as she went along. She taught what she called *"eurythmics,"* the free-style, graceful movement of the body in response to the rhythm of music. Louise loved it. She called it "inner rhythm." She would continue to study with Ellen Kearns for the next twenty years.

Perhaps the most important thing that Louise absorbed from Ellen was the ability to tap her inner strength —to regenerate her own energy.

> I question whether I'd have had the energy I have without studying with her. . . . Modern dance . . . makes you aware of movement, and that *moving* from the center of the being is where we generate and create our own energy.

She became aware of every part of her body, "and it freed me." She learned to do everything, even picking up a teacup, "as a creative act."[16]

DURING the summer of 1933, Marjorie Eaton returned to Taos and then went on to Mexico. In December, Frida and Diego also went back to Mexico. Louise suddenly found herself alone. The groups of people who were attracted to Diego no longer had a reason for coming, and the building was strangely quiet. Louise was truly on her own.

She intensified her study of dance with Ellen Kearns and convinced Lillian to take a dance class with her. She took occasional drawing classes at the Art Students League. Then, in April of 1934, she moved into a small studio on Tenth Street—in a building inhabited by many other artists. And she began to spend more time with Lillian and Ben.

It was at their home one evening that Louise met Chaim Gross, a talented young sculptor who was working then in wood and was teaching at the Educational Alliance. By this time Gross, only twenty-nine years old, had created works in thirty different types of wood and was considered a pioneer in the art of wood carving. Shortly after they met, Gross invited Louise to attend his class at the Alliance.

From him Louise had training in the techniques of sculpture, and soon she was producing work in terra cotta. This would be the beginning of her gradual transition from painter to sculptor. Gross offered her encouragement and even told her that her talent was evident the first night she attended his class.[17] Throughout his own career, happiness and optimism have suffused his work. No doubt he communicated some of this to Louise. She was beginning to feel good about herself.

"Energy can be imagined in patterns which change." Untitled
(left & right), **Night Form** *(center), cast stone.* FARNSWORTH
MUSEUM, GIFT OF THE ARTIST, 1981. PHOTO BY L. H. BOBER.

"I Am a Woman's Liberation"

THE THIRTIES was a difficult time for many people. By the beginning of 1933, the bottom had fallen out of the national economy. Many of the nation's banks had closed their doors, millions of people were unemployed, and hunger and destitution stalked the country.

Franklin Delano Roosevelt had just become president, and his *New Deal* had declared itself responsible for the welfare of every citizen. He proposed a massive program for public employment and received from Congress almost five billion dollars, the largest single appropriation in history. The program, called the Works Progress Administration (WPA), took shape in a multitude of new agencies. One of them, the Federal Arts Projects, was established in 1935 "to feed the hunger of millions for music, books, plays and pictures." [1]

The WPA provided financial support for about five thousand artists. Its programs gave artists materials, tools and a small salary. For this they were expected to bring a new work to the government art headquarters in their city every two to four weeks. These were evaluated and the best were sent to Washington to be shown there or sent on traveling exhibitions. It was these traveling exhibitions that exposed people all over the country to art. For many it was their first artistic or cultural experience. Perhaps most important, the WPA provided the opportunity for artists to do what they most needed to do—create. Men and women who would go on to become major American artists—Willem de Kooning, Mark Rothko, David Smith, Jackson Pollock—all got work on the project, and all received checks from the WPA that sustained them. It was these artists who would carry the United States to world leadership in the field of modern art.

Louise, though, was reluctant to join the program because she was receiving some help from her family. She didn't feel that she was entitled to participate. But the opportunity was far too enticing to pass up, and she did accept a position as an art teacher in March of 1935.

Her first assignment was to teach the principles of mural painting to the boys (aged nine to seventeen) at the Flatbush Boys' Club in Brooklyn. She taught them every day for six weeks. She approached the job with great trepidation—afraid and worried that she wouldn't be able to communicate with the boys. But it soon became "a great adventure," and she loved it. The boys "tackled mural painting . . . with such naturalness . . ." that she found it hard to call what she was doing *teaching*. She often couldn't remember a boy's name, but she recognized them all instantly by their work. The boys opened up a whole new world for her.

She began to think that she could be a good teacher:

"I, who could learn so little from dogmatic teaching, began by living the things I wanted to convey." She simply let the boys express themselves in a natural way. When she noticed that one of them always worked in dark, somber colors, one bright day she said to him, "Isn't it a beautiful light sunny day?" The message got across. Soon he showed her "a lovely light sunny picture."[2]

SHE CONTINUED to work independently as a painter and a sculptor also and to attend some of the many workshops for artists sponsored by the WPA. In one of these, she learned more about the techniques of sculpture. At a foundry she watched as they fired clay pieces, did plaster castings, and developed new techniques for casting in plaster and metal.[3]

She began to collect pieces of African sculpture. She liked, particularly, figures covered with cowrie shells, beads, raffia, and other objects of mysterious origin.[4]

DURING THESE YEARS Louise was invited to exhibit paintings and sculpture in several group shows at various New York galleries. Occasionally, Lillian exhibited some paintings with her. In 1935, Louise was in a show at the Brooklyn Museum entitled, "Young Sculptors." The following year she showed a sculpture in a competitive exhibition sponsored by the American Artist Congress at the A.C.A. Gallery on West Eighth Street in New York. The A.C.A. was referred to then as "the people's gallery," since they exhibited art whose themes were of concern to people.

When her work for the A.C.A. show received fine reviews in the New York newspapers, Louise's self-confidence soared. And when she was one of the four young artists selected from the show to give another exhibition, she was ecstatic.

She was surprised, though, that the work she had exhibited was mistakenly thought by some critics to be wood.

Now, at that time I did figures that were mostly painted plaster. . . . I was really searching for form. I painted each plane a different primary color so that the form would be as clear a line as architecture.[5]

She was working, she was experimenting with art forms, she was learning, but she was still living in relative poverty. And she was lonely. Other than her family, her work was her only constant companion. She seemed unable, or unwilling, to establish lasting friendships.

When her brother Nathan sent her "a few bucks," as he often did, he invariably implored her to use it for food and to "spend it in good health."[6] But she was content to have a piece of bread, a can of sardines, a cup of tea if she were hungry. She used the money he sent to buy paint. She taught herself not to waste and not to develop "fancy tastes, fancy appetites."[7]

"Who says you have to eat? Art is more important."[8]

But she never allowed herself to look like the "down-and-out artist." She continued to dress with the same flair she had exhibited back in high school. She recognized quickly that while it was "in" to call yourself *bohemian*, it "meant that you were enslaved in another way." And she refused to live where other artists lived—to be part of a group. For her, then as now, work was enough. "I'd rather work twenty-four hours a day—and then fall down on the bed than do anything I know. Because this is living." She knew, also, that being a woman wasn't going to stand in her way. She would compete in a man's world. She wouldn't play the role of looking pretty and throwing little handkerchiefs around. "If you play that role you don't build an empire."[9]

But she always felt feminine. She *knew* she was a glamorous and exciting woman who loved to dress up and to have fun. She knew that women can have physical strength and mental creativity and still be feminine. She knew, also, that she would be a great artist. She had the talent. She would find the courage. She had to. She had long ago made the choice to dedicate herself to her art. She wasn't about to give up now. But she would remain a lady.

Perhaps this is why, years later, when she was questioned about her reaction to the women's movement, she could reply, "I *am* a woman's liberation."[10]

She took comfort from the knowledge that Mike was happy in Rockland. He was learning from his grandfather and from his uncle Nate how to handle wood, how to build furniture, how to make frames. He was rapidly becoming a skilled wood craftsman. And he was beginning to study for his *Bar Mitzvah*, the religious ceremony at which a thirteen-year-old boy becomes an adult member of the Jewish community. Later Mike celebrated his *Bar Mitzvah* at Temple Emanu-El in New York City.

When Louise sent him the traditional gift of his own *talis*, or prayer shawl, for the occasion, he wrote to her:

> I want to thank you for the "talis," it is very beautiful and is just what I needed.

In the same letter he described a blizzard so severe that the wind forced cracks in the walls and the snow came into the house. Louise was glad that she was in New York, although she was planning to visit Rockland soon.

Mike ended his letter with a message from Minna: "Gramma [sic] just said for you to dress human when you come up here." But, as always, he was concerned that she was spending her money on him and cautioned her to "take care of yourself." [11]

Mike kept her informed of all his activities: "Every afternoon I go to *Hadah* [Hebrew School]." He joined the Rockland Boy Scouts, and he asked for a guitar. Then he decided, "I perfectly agree with you fully now and would like to take piano lessons when back in good old New York City."

But his dreams of living with his mother in New York would have to wait. Mike was sent to Peekskill Military Academy, which his father seemed to feel would be good for him. (Over the years Louise and Charles kept in touch with each other about Mike. Charles wrote to Louise whenever he saw Mike and told her frequently how proud he was of "our son.")

Mike was lonesome at the Academy and begged his mother to write to him and to visit him. One weekend when Louise did visit him there she showed him a block of wood that she carried in her bag to work on at odd moments. He was fascinated as he watched her carving a primitive oceanic figure from it. Finally, in September of 1936, when Louise was living in a studio on Bleeker Street, Mike came to New York to attend Stuyvesant High School and to live with her. Shortly afterwards they moved to East Fifteenth Street, and then, in the summer of 1939, they rented a three-room railroad flat at 311 East Twenty-first

Street. Louise, worried that Mike didn't have the advantages of her mother's house in Rockland, insisted that he take the only room that had a degree of fresh air and sunlight. She would work elsewhere in the apartment with artificial light.

When Mike graduated from Stuyvesant High School in 1940, he enrolled in New York University. But his stay there was brief. Early in 1941, he returned to Maine and then, that spring, he joined the Merchant Marine. It was to be the beginning of a long period of sailing merchant ships around the world. His mother was devastated.

Alone, financially destitute (the W.P.A. program had ended in 1939), and emotionally drowning, she struggled frantically to find meaning in her work. She had sacrificed everything for her art. Had she made the wrong choice?

Then, in August, a distant cousin arrived in New York and invited her to have dinner with him at the Plaza Hotel. It had been a long time since Louise had had a decent meal, even longer since she'd been to an elegant hotel, but she did have an outfit she could wear. She accepted the invitation. It was a beautiful warm summer evening, so after dinner her cousin hired a car and driver to take them to Montauk, Long Island.[12]

The next day Louise suddenly realized that while she could barely sustain herself, her cousin had spent a thousand dollars in two days. The shock of the extravagance was the jolt she needed. She was determined now that somehow she would be recognized with a show of her work, and it would have to be at the best gallery in New York. This, she felt, was the Nierendorf Gallery on East Fifty-seventh Street, just a few blocks from the Plaza Hotel. Karl Nierendorf had fled Nazi Germany some years before and had opened a gallery in New York shortly after he arrived there. It rapidly gained a reputation as the best gallery of modern art in the city. Among the artists whose work he exhibited were Picasso, Matisse and Paul Klee.

So Louise walked to the gallery, introduced herself to Mr. Nierendorf, and then startled him by announcing,

"I want an exhibition in your gallery, Mr. Nierendorf."

"But I don't know your work."

"Well, you can come and see my work."

"Where do you live?"

"Three-eleven East Twenty-first Street."

Intrigued by the boldness of this beautiful woman, Nierendorf agreed to come to her house the next evening.

All the work that Louise had done on the WPA project was stored in the cellar of the building she was living in. It was this that she showed him when he arrived. Louise knew that galleries generally plan their shows about a year in advance, but she refused to allow herself even to think about this. Nierendorf studied the pieces thoughtfully for a few minutes, then said quietly, "You can have a show in three weeks." Somehow, Louise was not surprised.

"I think we create our lives. I'm not going to accept words like *luck* and *break*. . . ."[13]

During the next two weeks Louise selected the pieces she wanted to show, then worked feverishly, cleaning and repainting them. On September 22, 1941, her first one-woman show opened at the Nierendorf Gallery. And it was a first for Karl Nierendorf also. It was his first exhibition of an American artist.

The show was reviewed by all the major art critics. One infuriated her: "We learned the artist is a woman, in time to check our enthusiasm. Had it been otherwise we might have hailed these sculptural expressions as by surely a great figure among moderns."[14] But the review in *The New York Times* began:

> Modern indeed are the forms and rhythms employed by Louise Nevelson. . . . The artist makes her line felt even when employing heavy low masses that at times are reminiscent of Mayan and certain Near Eastern work.

It concluded: ". . . Miss Nevelson has originality and a rather personal approach . . . and has made an interesting start."[15]

Another review in the *New York Herald Tribune* spoke of "wit and a feeling of the primitive in her work," the "suggestions of the mysticism of ancient Mexican art," and "a dancing figure that symbolizes a zestful interest in movement. The work is well off the beaten track, a little mannered, and cleverly done."[16] Another spoke of their rigidity and their movement as "a coiled spring might be."[17] In fact, the response to the exhibit was so great that Karl Nierendorf extended the showing and held a reception so she would have an opportunity to meet "interesting people."

Her unique style and the influence of pre-Columbian art and of the movement of dance had already made a subtle impact on her art.

But there were no sales.

───────⬥─⬥───────

KARL NIERENDORF left on a business trip to California, and Louise moved from the house on Twenty-first Street to a huge loft on East Tenth Street. The rent was only fifteen dollars a month. But she was alone in a four-story building, cold and miserable. For weeks she did nothing but lie in bed.

"I saw darkness for weeks." But "nature heals you, and you do come out of it. All of a sudden I saw a crack of light. . . . Then I saw forms in the light. And I recognized that there was no darkness, that in darkness there'll always be light." [18]

Perhaps it was the friendship with Karl Nierendorf that was beginning to develop that helped her to see that light. He wrote to her from Hollywood, telling her how disappointed he was that he hadn't received a letter from her. He understood, though, he told her, "how much of an effort it needs to say something in written language what would be so simple to express personally . . . I wish you were here." [19]

His concern for her was evident. When he returned he continued to offer her encouragement and emotional support. "I know Picasso and Matisse," he told her. "I know all the great artists. I know how they move. You're going to be great also. You're going to have every desire in creativity fulfilled." [20]

She wanted to believe him.

WHEN SHE started to work again she realized one day that she was working only in black, and that her work was all enclosed. "I couldn't think of doing a piece in the round." There was "a place of great secrecy within myself." [21] Mike was in the war (the United States had entered the Second World War in December, 1941), his missions were often secret and she didn't hear from him for months at a time. When a letter did arrive it was often censored. Parts of it, giving her an address where she could write to him, were cut out, increasing her frustration. Her fear, her loneliness, her despair were reflected in her sculpture. Her work became, for her, a way of trying to understand the world.

And she began to use found objects.

I had all this wood lying around, and I began to compose. Anywhere I found wood, I took it home and started working with it.[22]

Her next show at Nierendorf's, in October of 1942, brought more praise from the critics. Reviews spoke of her vitality, her originality, her humor.

"A World of Geometry and Magic"

FROM THE TIME back in 1926, when Louise had first attended classes at the Theatre Arts Institute in Brooklyn she had maintained contact with its founder and director, Friederich Kiesler. Over the years Kiesler had occasionally discussed with Louise his exciting new ideas on sculpture, theater design and architecture. His renowned sense of humor sometimes helped to raise her gloomy spirits.

Perhaps the most important thing that Kiesler did for Louise, though, was to introduce her to many of the exciting artists who were at that time exiled in the United States as a result of Nazism and World War II. Through Kiesler, Louise met poet and critic André Breton, the leading spokesman of the surrealist movement in New York; Max Ernst, considered by many the most inventive painter of the surrealists; Marcel Duchamp; and Piet Mondrian, the Dutch abstract painter.

Mondrian became a special friend. At seventy years of age he was still a very fine dancer, and he and Louise loved to go dancing together. She was intrigued by the simplicity of his life—he lived alone and kept his studio immaculate. "He *cleaned* everything, even in life . . . He measured his emotions just as he would make a painting," Louise said of him.[1]

Mondrian's style was severe: he restricted his design to horizontals and verticals and his colors to the three primary hues—red, blue, and yellow, plus black and white. His paintings would exert a subtle influence on Louise's art.

Kiesler also introduced Louise to Peggy Guggenheim,* who was to play an important role in the flourishing of modern art in America. Peggy was a very wealthy New Yorker who had just returned from fourteen years in Europe. There, her friend Marcel Duchamp had introduced her to many of the artists who were working in Paris at the time. Duchamp taught her the difference between abstract and surrealist art and gave her a "shopping list" as a guide to help her in her resolve to "buy a picture a day." Seemingly oblivious to the war that was raging around her, Peggy bought works by Picasso, Braque, Kandinsky and Mondrian. She acquired Brancusi's sculpture *Bird in Space* as the Germans were marching on Paris. Only then did she decide that she had better go home.

Although the Nazis had forbidden that any artwork leave France, somehow Peggy Guggenheim managed to outwit them and to smuggle her paintings out. She simply took them off their stretchers and packed them in cases with her linens and blankets. Then she labeled the boxes "household objects" and shipped them back to America.[2]

When Peggy returned to New York she convinced

* The Guggenheim Museum, in the magnificent spiral building on Fifth Avenue in Manhattan designed by Frank Lloyd Wright, was created by Peggy's uncle, Solomon R. Guggenheim.

Kiesler to design a museum for her. In October 1942, her Art of the Century Gallery opened at 30 West Fifty-seventh Street. Kiesler's unusual design and the art in the museum —which included pieces Peggy had brought from Europe —caused a stir in the art world. The work of artists from England, France, Germany and Holland were represented. Too, many of these artists were fleeing war-torn Europe, seeking refuge in the United States. As they drew from their own rich cultural heritages they produced works of art that had exciting new themes. Through Kiesler, Louise could watch them all from a front row seat.

THE SAME MONTH that Peggy Guggenheim's Gallery opened saw Louise's second exhibit at Nierendorf's. This time the beautiful outfit she wore to the opening was not something hastily put together from the back of her closet. It was a gift from Karl Nierendorf. In just one year he had become her dealer, her adviser, her friend.

At the opening night party Louise, radiant, glowing, was introduced to the American sculptor David Smith, who had brought along his young friend Ralph Rosenborg. Ralph was immediately drawn to Louise, and when the gallery closed that evening he escorted her home. And so began "one of the longest romances of her life."[3]

Ralph was a gifted painter in his own right. He was twenty-nine when he and Louise met, but he was already displaying the sensitivity and perception, the unerring sense of his craft that would bring him recognition as an artist whose small watercolors and oils have been called a "lyric celebration of the beauties of nature."[4]

Ralph loved wood also, and he knew how to use it. He

taught Louise how to use dowels, and together they made frames for her collection of Eilshemius paintings. She had recently begun to collect the work of this painter, whom she described as a lonely man and a fine artist. She loved the color and vitality of his work and wanted to own some of it although Eilshemius had not yet become a recognized artist. Ralph encouraged her also to pursue the art of wood sculpture.

ABOUT A MONTH LATER, in the atmosphere of surrealism that was permeating the New York art scene at that time,* Louise had what she called a "landmark" occurrence in her life. One dreary November morning she was walking on Tenth Street, on her way uptown to the Metropolitan Museum of Art. It was just beginning to snow, she recalls, and the city looked "gray-opaque." All of a sudden, cutting through the gray, she saw yellow, "and it's so yellow that it makes everything (else) recede."[5]

As she stared at it she realized that what she was looking at was a little old man carrying a yellow shoeshine box under his arm. Impulsively, she ran after him.

"You have a beautiful shoeshine box."

"Thank you."

"Do you want to sell it?"

"No."

Then, in his broken English he told her that his name was Joe Milone, he shined shoes for a living, and he had been on that corner with his shoeshine box for years and

---

* Surrealism, Louise said of that time, "was in the air."

no one had ever noticed him before. Then he went on, "If you like this box you come here Monday and I'll show you the most beautiful shoeshine stand in the world."

On Monday morning Joe Milone did arrive as promised with "the most beautiful object in the world . . . (a) superbly elegant work of art . . . the essence of surrealism. Purely imaginative art without forethought or conclusion." The entire stand, made in five pieces, was completely encrusted with ornaments Joe Milone had been collecting for ten years—many-colored beads, iridescent buttons, glass door knobs, bells, costume jewelry, a gilt cupid, painted iron flowers, ribbon rosettes—all gathered over the years from pushcarts and five-and-ten-cent stores.[6]

Louise, overwhelmed by the sight of this jeweled shoe stand, this "throne" for the customer to sit on, asked him, "Would you permit me to take this to the Museum of Modern Art?"

"Anything," he answered.[7]

So Louise phoned the curator of the museum, Dorothy Miller, whom she had recently met, and told her, "Dorothy, I have something for the museum." Then she took Joe Milone and his box in a truck uptown to Fifty-third Street. When the museum's director, Alfred Barr, saw the box he decided that since it was just before Christmas, "We'll give the city a Christmas present. We'll put it on exhibition in the lobby."

The experience left an indelible impression on Louise. She recognized that Joe Milone was a simple, pure and honest man whose sensitivity had enabled him to create a work of art simply out of his desire to find beauty.

But when Karl Nierendorf asked her, "Nevelson, what made you go to the museum?" she could reply matter-of-factly, "Where am I supposed to go with it?"[8]

BY THE BEGINNING of 1943, Louise had made many new friends, she was involved in the "art world" and was aware of almost everything that was going on. She was following closely the career of Martha Graham and of Isamu Noguchi, the young Japanese-American sculptor who often designed sets for Martha Graham's dances. And she was working prodigiously. Karl Nierendorf arranged for showings all around the country so that people outside of New York had an opportunity to see her work. She showed paintings and sculptures in numerous New York galleries. Her work was in Peggy Guggenheim's exhibition: *Thirty-one Women*. In February, her entry of a child's wooden seat won a prize in the Museum of Modern Art's *Arts in Therapy*. (Since her work on the Federal Arts Project Louise had maintained a vital interest in children's art.) For this exhibit, held as a benefit to raise money for wounded war veterans, artists submitted new designs and objects that might be used in art therapy.[9]

Then, in a cruel blow that she could barely endure, Louise lost her mother. Minna had been ill frequently throughout her life, and she had rarely been happy. Her final illness kept her in Lowell, Massachusetts, General Hospital for two months, until she passed away there in March, 1943. Louise felt abandoned. Her bright and beautiful mother, whom she adored, and whose love and faith and understanding had sustained her through years of groping, of misery and loneliness, was gone. She couldn't talk about it—she couldn't even bring herself to attend the funeral. The only way she knew to vent her silent raging grief was to immerse herself even more deeply in her work.

Soon she found herself composing day and night—

wearing cotton clothes so she could work in them or sleep in them. She worked until she was physically exhausted, seldom stopping for food—unwilling to "waste" time eating. Nothing mattered except the work.

Then, in April, she became a frequent sight on Fifty-seventh Street wearing one of her floppy, broad-brimmed hats and long pants under her skirt, tunic style. Even in April she was always cold. She was going back and forth between the Norlyst Gallery and Nierendorf's. She had two shows at once!

Her exhibit at the Norlyst Gallery, which had recently been opened by friends of Friederich Kiesler, was entitled *Circus: The Clown is the Center of His World.** Some of her first efforts in wood—pieces Ralph Rosenborg had encouraged her to do—were included in this exhibit.

There were three groups of figures: animals, clowns, and the people looking on, set against a background of ancient circus posters. There were funny clowns, trapeze artists, and whimsical animals made of all kinds of scrap material. Some even had eyes made of multicolored electric light bulbs. The animals were designed as art objects, but they could also be used as moveable blocks for children to play with. Louise hoped that as the children played with the fishes and the seals as though they were blocks, they would *see* the different forms and recognize their relationship to one another. In spite of her submerged grief, her sense of fun continued to express itself in her art.

But this show wasn't enough for her. She had talked Karl Nierendorf into giving her a show of drawings at the same time—"to balance" the sculpture show. She needed

* Perhaps Martha Graham's successful dance piece, *Every Soul is a Circus*, first performed in New York in December, 1939, had exerted a subtle influence on her.[10]

the two exhibitions at once—and the work necessary to get ready for them. She could busy herself in her work—forget her grief for the moment—and compose.

Both shows were acclaimed by the critics. This time *Cue* Magazine called her a "sculptor bursting with youth, energy and a touch that brings all things to life." Of her paintings (portraits) the reviewer wrote: ". . . her color-loaded brush . . . on big canvases . . . make(s) a glad song."[11] No longer did they mock her as a woman.

But still nothing sold.

At the conclusion of each of the shows her work was returned to her. She didn't know what to do with it. She had no place to keep it. She found herself becoming angrier and angrier, and in one final burst of anger she just took two hundred paintings off their stretchers and burned them. Then she burned the entire Circus, and later gave her wood-carving tools to Mike.

"All my life people have told me not to waste my energies on anger, but I kept anger, I tapped it and tapped it. Anger has given me great strength."[12]

In spite of her anger, though, Louise never questioned that what she was doing was right. She continued to work. She was "like a racehorse with blinders. I didn't know you could change in midstream. I kept going."[13]

A letter from Mike that arrived at this time touched her deeply. Mike told his mother to withdraw money from his bank account (his pay from the United States Government for his service in the Merchant Marine) to pay for her food and her rent. She mustn't use it for artist's supplies, though. Mike knew his mother well! He explained that she could continue to use his money for as long as the war lasted. After that, when he returned home, he would need it to pay for his education.[14]

Whimsical fishes and seals that children could play with as though they were blocks. "Wondrous Fishes and Balancing Seals" from **Circus: The Clown Is the Center of His World,** *1942–43, wood, destroyed.* SMITHSONIAN INSTITUTION.

WHEN LOUISE did make a trip back to Rockland to visit her family, Nate asked her what she would like of the small inheritance their mother had left. Louise told him that what she wanted more than anything else was a house of her own in New York. Nate, financially successful himself in Rockland, and always happy to give his sister whatever he could, agreed to buy one for her. She was overjoyed.

It was good to be with them—to soak up the warmth of their presence, of their caring for her. It was good, also, to walk through the town and the outlying areas with her father and see the many houses he had built over the years. It was with great pride that he showed her his "personal empire."

Within a week after Louise returned to New York her friend Ralph Rosenborg found a house for her. At the time, Ralph was living on the corner of Lexington Avenue and Thirtieth Street. He walked east on Thirtieth Street one day and found a beautiful seventy-year-old brownstone for sale. Louise loved it at once. The house had four stories plus a cellar and a backyard that she could work in for a good part of the year. The rooms were long and narrow, with very high ceilings—and there were seven marble fireplaces!

Immediately Louise saw what had to be done. All the lessons she had learned from her father when she was a little girl and he had taken her to look at houses with him in Rockland came flooding back now. She remembered also his teaching that a small corner must be left unfinished. This would be a fitting legacy. And almost as quickly as she could describe to Ralph what changes she envisioned in the house, he could execute them. They moved walls, changed ceilings, enlarged rooms. Her energy knew no bounds. They made a studio of the entire first floor. There was plenty of space for storage in the basement, and the top floors were kept for friends and relatives who came to stay. Occasionally she rented some of those rooms in an effort to derive income. Her first tenant was Peggy Guggenheim, who took the entire two top floors. Peggy's only requirement was that Louise install a large refrigerator and a gas range so she could cook and entertain there. She paid Louise three hundred dollars a month.[15]

Since Louise had left Rockland as a bride she had lived in twelve different places in New York. This would be for her, her first real home—the house in Manhattan she had yearned for for so many years. She named it "The Farm," becuase of the red barn that bordered the property facing the garden in the back.

She furnished the house with modern furniture, but with tapestries and Oriental rugs as well. She hung the paintings that she and Ralph had framed, and displayed her collection of African sculptures that she had been accumulating over the years.

In the garden she "planted" rows of cooking utensils— eggbeaters, spatulas, wooden spoons painted black, saying, "that's what you do with them."[16] (She rarely cooked at home.) Her sense of humor was reasserting itself. Then she attached pieces of discarded wood to the barn wall and made a mural of found objects. Finally, she put mirrors in the ground to reflect the sky. Now, using the stone ledge in the garden as a table, she could work in her own "environment" almost eight months of the year.

And she continued to work. In 1944, she had her first exhibition of abstract wood assemblages at Nierendorf's Gallery. Then, in 1946, she showed a group of small wooden sculptures that together represented an "Ancient City." It would be her last exhibit with Karl Nierendorf.

In 1947, just after his return from a long business trip to Germany, Karl Nierendorf phoned Louise to say hello and to ask her to come to the gallery in a few days to plan her next show. She was glad he was back. She had missed him. He had gone to Europe for two weeks (his first trip since World War II had ended) and stayed a year and a half! She had realized while he was gone how much she had come to depend on him. She was the only American artist who showed with him on a permanent basis. She was the only woman who ever showed with him. He had never denied her any request she had made of him, and she had begun to think of him as her spiritual godfather.

The night before the scheduled appointment a friend phoned Louise to tell her that Karl Nierendorf was dead. Louise was stunned. She refused to believe it. The night became an agony of waiting. The next morning, newspaper reports confirmed the story. Louise was devastated. She went into a state of severe depression.

Louise remained despondent and inactive for several months. She was unable to work. She couldn't believe that Nierendorf was gone. Soon she began to realize that her general feeling of depression was more than emotional. There was a physical problem gnawing at her as well. A tumor was discovered and (in 1948) she underwent surgery to have it removed. Later that year her sister Anita, in the hope of hastening her recuperation, suggested that they go to Europe. The two sisters made a brief trip to England, France and Italy, and Louise returned still weak, but refreshed and ready to work again.

Concerned friends, who recognized that she would be unable to handle heavy wood pieces now, suggested that

Louise work in ceramics at the Sculpture Center, a combination school, workshop and gallery for sculptors on Eighth Street. Anyone interested in sculpture could work there in clay, stone or metal. Space and assistance were always available. Annual group shows at the Center often included the sculptors David Smith, Alexander Calder, Jose de Rivera and Isamu Noguchi.

So began a period of intense productivity. In the next two years Louise made hundreds of pieces—mostly in terra cotta. One series, entitled *Moving-Static-Moving-Figures*, was a group of pieces made up of geometric forms and torsos, stacked on wooden dowels that allowed them to turn and so to change relationships. Louise achieved a textured finish on the clay by pressing fabric into it while it was still wet. Then she drew stylized faces on the surface with a sharp tool. When she finished, the pieces looked much like relics of an ancient world.[17] Once again, her interest in pre-Columbian art was evident. But she still couldn't bring herself to establish a relationship with another gallery.

In Rockland, Nate and Anita were still worried about their sister "Lou." So (in October, 1949) Anita made another trip to New York and stayed with Louise for a while. While Anita was there, Louise's conversation seemed to turn more and more to Mexican art and to Diego Rivera and the work she had done with him. Anita quickly decided to take advantage of this reawakening interest—she offered Louise a trip to Mexico. Her gift was twofold. She would keep Louise company, and she would pay all expenses. Louise was overjoyed.

Spring of 1950 found the two sisters traveling together once again—this time on a plane bound for Mexico City. There they did visit Frida and Diego Rivera. But they found that Frida was in the hospital and Diego was living alone in the blue adobe house that had been the home of the Kahlo family before he and Frida had met and married. Anita and Louise were fascinated with the furnishings that reflected Frida's interest in colonial Mexico. They loved the kitchen garden that Frida had tended. Diego's passion for Indian artifacts was evident too—in the many pieces of pre-Columbian sculpture and pottery throughout the house. And they enjoyed visiting with Frida. Despite the fact that she was in the hospital and knew that she was dying, she and Diego were both cheerful and outwardly happy. Louise was glad she had the opportunity to spend time with them. It would be the last time she would see them. Frida died of cancer in 1954 at the age of 47, Diego of a heart ailment three years later.

Louise and Anita saw the museums in Mexico City. Then they traveled to the Yucatan, the most interesting archeological region in Mexico, to see the ruins of the ancient Mayan civilization. The Maya were people of Mexico and Central America who had developed a high form of civilization in the New World before the arrival of the white man. Their descendants have survived in the Yucatan and in the highlands of Guatemala. Perhaps the Indian culture she was seeing here brought back memories of the Indians she had known as a child in Maine.

Louise and Anita visited the cities of Uxmal and Chichen Itza in Yucatan. There the ancient temples and palaces overwhelmed them:

> Yucatan was a world of forms that at once I felt was mine, a world where East and West met, a world of geometry and magic.[18]

Her feeling for pre-Columbian art was intensifying. They returned to Mexico City via Oaxaca, then headed back to New York City. A few months later found them back in Central America, this time visiting Guatemala. Here, in Copan and Guirigua, they saw stone-built cities— or "ceremonial centers"—composed of pyramids and platforms grouped around large open courts. Louise would say of these trips:

> According to my book, Mexico and its sculpture and pyramids is number one. It will stand up to anything on this earth.[19]

The Yucatan provided a rich visual feast that would remain with her forever, intensifying as she reflected on it over the years, and juxtaposed it in her mind's eye against the exciting but very different architecture of modern Manhattan.

AS SOON as they returned to New York Anita knew that her instinct to take her sister to Mexico had been a good one. Louise came back fired with enthusiasm to work again —determined to make a name for herself in the art world —and to make a financial success of her art as well.

She began to think that to be considered great, an artist had to produce and exhibit tremendous quantities of work. "I'll flood the market with my work 'til they know I'm here,"[20] she decided. She attended art openings, she participated in group shows, she joined artists' groups and she offered her home as a meeting place for many of them.

One group, known as *The Four O'Clock Forum*, met there every Sunday afternoon at four P.M. Artists such as Willem de Kooning, Max Weber, Mark Rothko and Marcel Duchamp all came and shared their views on art. It was an exciting time and Louise was at the center of it.

She continued to sculpt in terra cotta, and she worked for a time at Atelier 17,* a studio established by the English artist Stanley William Hayter for etching. She had worked there briefly some years before, but had not liked the tools. "I can't stand these tools . . . I'm not a dentist," she had said then.[21]

Now, she tried a can opener instead of the prescribed tools. Then one day when she saw a white lace curtain blowing in a breeze, she suddenly recognized in its "gossamer quality, (its) reflection, (its) form, (its) movement"[22]— the exciting possibilities for etching.** She used the can opener and etched a piece of lace into a copper plate. She was thrilled as she watched the transformation of the plate in the acid and saw the lacy design appear on it. Louise had found her own way to use the medium—to give it her distinctive stamp. In one month she made thirty etchings. Ultimately she would give these plates to the Museum of Modern Art.

* An atelier is a studio where a master not only employs but instructs his students. The atelier plan originated in France.

** "An etching is made by coating a copper plate with resin to make an acid-resistant 'ground,' through which the design is scratched with a needle, laying bare the metal surface underneath. The plate is then bathed in an acid that etches ('bites') the lines into the copper."[23]

Boxes and Compartments: Jars of Colored Candy Remembered

BY 1954, New York was experiencing a postwar economic boom (World War II had ended in 1945) and its streets were littered with discarded wood, crates and furniture. There was a spurt of building, with the result that lumber yards were springing up all over in order to meet the demand for wood to construct the houses.

At the same time Louise was finding it more and more difficult to handle the rising cost of clay for her sculpture. But she had to create—and to her the act was more important than the material. Gradually, she found herself rummaging through the piles of wood she often saw stacked up outside her house or in the scrap piles of lumber yards nearby. One day she saw a long narrow box that might have contained a rolled-up rug. That's beautiful, she thought, so she picked it up and took it back to her studio. Soon she began to see other marvelous things in the streets. She would pick out a few pieces, then drag the wood home and sort it out according to shape, size, texture.

She began to feel that the wood was alive—that she could communicate with it. It had a "livingness." Her mind raced back to the little girl she had been in Rockland—walking on the beach, searching for bits of driftwood that had been washed up onto the shore; the wood stacked in her father's lumberyard; going with him to look at houses —even watching him build them; the trees that seemed to be everywhere in Maine.

Soon she had friends and family roving the streets searching for choice fragments of wood. They were different forms and shapes—some even had nails and nail holes in them. But she just nailed them together—and *knew* this was art. So she began to learn more about the technique.

The wood seemed to act as fuel for her engine, and in a burst of creative energy, she began working feverishly. "I had this energy that was flowing like an ocean into creativity . . . I identify with the ocean."[1] She had always been impatient. Now she had a fast way of saying what she wanted to say. Wood allowed her to work quickly.

As she looked for ways to use the wood to convey new meaning in her work she thought, "If I paint the pieces black, I'll be better able to see their form—without any distractions." So she donned an old pair of gloves, and using her kitchen tongs to hold the wood, dipped each piece into a can of matte black paint. Then she let them dry. Suddenly, the forms had taken on a feeling of *greatness*.

She began to use the wood to make what she would later call *table-top landscapes*. One of these, *Black Majesty*, revealed anew her strong feeling for African art. Then,

Two *"table-top landscapes."* **Black Majesty,** *its different shapes unified by a coat of black paint, reflects Nevelson's feeling for Africa.* **East River City Scape** *illustrates her love of the Manhattan skyline.* **Black Majesty,** *1955, painted wood.* WHITNEY MUSEUM OF AMERICAN ART. **East River City Scape,** *1956, wood painted black.* WEATHERSPOON ART GALLERY. UNIVERSITY OF NORTH CAROLINA AT GREENSBORO.

inspired by the silhouette of the Manhattan skyline at dusk, she made a series of city scapes from the wood fragments. *East River City Scape* reflected the geometry and rhythm that she saw and loved in New York's urban architecture.

It was just at this time that Louise was notified by the city of New York that her house, along with all the others in the area, would be torn down in order to build the Kips Bay Housing Project, a group of twenty-one-story apartment buildings designed by the architect I. M. Pei between Thirtieth and Thirty-third Streets, from First to Second Avenue. Louise would have to find another place to live. She was devastated. But she did nothing about it. She simply continued to work.

One of the group shows in which Louise had participated in 1953 took place at the Grand Central Moderns Gallery. Then gradually, over the next two years, a friendly relationship built up between Louise and Colette Roberts, director of the Gallery. In 1955, Louise formed an exclusive association with Grand Central Moderns, her first since her friend Karl Nierendorf had died eight years before.[2]

Ancient Games and *Ancient Places* was her first one-woman exhibition there. She called it "ancient" because she wanted it to be timeless. Included in this show were the table-top landscapes she had been doing. Also in the exhibit were terra cotta pieces mounted on black bakelite bases that reflected the strong influence her trip to Mexico had had on her.[3] *Royal Voyages*, which marked the beginning of her uniform use of black, and *Forest*, reminiscent of her childhood in Maine, followed soon after.[4]

In September of 1955, Louise was asked by the Great Neck, New York, Public School System to teach an experimental sculpture workshop in their adult education program. She had several classes. One was organized as a beginning course for those interested in sculpture simply as a means of expression. Another was a creative workshop in which advanced students experimented with various materials. During the day Louise also held a parent-child workshop to encourage experimentation with different sculpting forms such as figures or abstracts.

As the students came to class, Louise greeted them at the door, telling them, "Leave your brain outside, sweetie." She encouraged them to keep their minds open and empty —"so when you see something, you see it *totally*." She advised them *not* to remember every name, address, telephone number. She told them that just as she regularly cleans her house, she cleans her mind:

> I take my mind out and put it on the table. I take
> silver polish or whatever and rags and sponges and
> clean it up and clear it up and keep it shiny.[5]

"Don't keep things in your head that you don't need," she cautioned.

Then she would let them work on their sculpture while she watched. She recognized that the environment was important for these students—the energy and consciousness that were pooled—the quiet communication among themselves.

Occasionally Louise gave a demonstration on a student's piece. With all the students gathered around her she would "take a knife and cut and give them planes and show them that this plane and that was like building an architectural building."[6] Perhaps here Louise was unconsciously imitating Hans Hofmann's method of teaching in Munich and at the Art Students League in New York years before, when he would choose a student's drawing to "rework" and ask the class to watch him.

The students loved her class. "You relieve us of the tensions of everyday living," they told her. And she tried to instill in each of them a sense of confidence, a "sense of self," and the courage to "take what belongs to them." She told them to write their names over and over every day and to be sure to sign their work.

An artist, she has said, is born with certain equipment, like a machine. You can take that equipment and you can put it where it's going to get rusty. But if you polish it and keep it going, it can last forever. If you have talent, you have to work. But you must believe in yourself. And you have to *want* to do it. "An artist," she said, "has to *live* like an artist, and then you *are* an artist. That's the point. No one is giving diplomas for being an artist."[7]

She left each evening exhausted but exhilarated. She knew that she was conveying to these students her own strong conviction that the world of art was at once exciting and important. And it was becoming more and more exciting for Louise.

IN NEW YORK, as the buildings all around her on Thirtieth Street were sold to the city and vacated, Louise remained in her house and composed. And she continued to collect wood. Ironically, though, as more and more wood remnants—chair backs, brush handles, weathered planking, architectural scroll work, even sweepings of chips and slivers from the carpenter's floor—found their way into her home, she began to run out of space to store it all. The wood, she realized, was marching in and taking over her home, her life. So she began to dispose of her own furniture. One by one she threw away chairs, tables, chests, until finally all that remained were her bed, her pillow, and her warm Hudson Bay blanket.[8]

Still, she was constantly on the lookout for more wood. As she walked, she had an uncanny knack for seeing around corners and behind things. Like an animal stalking its prey, she sought out fragments whose shape and texture appealed to her. Soon her kitchen, too, was piled high with black wood—in stark contrast to the red enameled refrigerator that had somehow escaped being tossed on the junk heap along with her other possessions. Even some of her bathtubs were filled with wood! A startled friend, coming to visit her one day, exclaimed, "This isn't a studio, it's a whole world!"[9]

But she needed working space, room to step back and *see* what she was doing. So she began to stack the pieces one on top of the other. Soon she realized what was happening. The wood pieces that she was stacking and arranging were becoming compositions. The walls of her house were their frames. Subtle relationships were forming among them. She recognized a rhythm in them. What had begun as a space-saving device had become a new form of creating.

Walking along Second Avenue one day, Louise noticed some discarded empty liquor cases stacked up outside a store, waiting to be carted away by the garbage collector. As she approached them, an idea began to take hold. She gathered up as many as she could carry and took them home. Quickly, she began placing pieces of wood inside them. She seemed to know exactly which pieces of wood to choose from her seemingly inexhaustible supply. Then she ran back and dragged home another load. Excitement was running through her now like electricity. She felt charged. She couldn't move fast enough.

> If you're going fast, you're not letting the conscious mind do so much thinking . . . So you're tapping everything, like a gold mine . . . So I use speed . . . this great energy takes you into new areas.[10]

She worked with such intense concentration that nothing else mattered. She thought of nothing else. She seemed to have an inner vision that was guiding her hands and giving her strength. She never stopped to measure. She kept moving. "I moved mountains." But the excitement, the love of the work "took the weight out of it." Her instinct for the placement of the boxes, for which shapes to repeat and where to repeat them and how to break their sequence was sure. Perhaps, while her conscious mind was not thinking, somewhere deep in the recesses of her subconscious mind she saw again the rows of glass jars filled with colored candy and stacked on the shelves in the depot in Liverpool, the scene that had so delighted her when she was a little girl.

It was only afterwards that she could step back, look at what she had done, and make an intelligent judgment about how to modify it. Only then could her trained eye evaluate her creation.

"The shadow is as important as the object." **Sky Cathedral,** 1958, *wood construction painted black.* MUSEUM OF MODERN ART, GIFT OF MR. AND MRS. BEN MILDWOLFF.

And she saw that she had moved into a "new area." As she stacked and placed the boxes at right angles to one another she noticed the way the light came through the cracks in the boxes and seemed to change the shape of the objects she was placing inside. Then she saw that by moving the boxes—setting them at different angles—she could create different shadows. She saw, too, how even cracks in the wood sucked in shadows. Suddenly she knew that "the shadow . . . is as important as the object." She would give it "as strong a form as the material object that gives me the shadow."[11] Her mysterious world of shadow boxes was born.

She named her first stacked wall *Cathedral in the Sky*, then went on to create a large group of *Assemblages* that together formed an "environment" that she called *Moon Garden + One*. Colette Roberts exhibited it in her gallery in February, 1958.

Moon Garden + One was truly an "environment." When Louise arrived at the gallery to supervise the installation of her work she was disturbed by the desk and chair that were there as part of the gallery. Still wrapped in her heavy black wool coat with its big fur collar to protect her from the chill winds of winter in Manhattan, she immediately asked Colette to have the furniture removed. "I didn't want . . . anything to intrude on the environment."[12]

She covered the windows with paper to block out the light, then set a piece of sculpture on one windowsill, using the window as its frame. She left the second window empty. The remaining pieces of sculpture were placed on the walls. Finally, the entire room was bathed in a dusky blue light that seemed to intensify the shadows. She had "*composed* the whole thing. . . . It was a feast—for my-self."[13]

Louise stood in the center of this *sculptured land-scape*, her moon garden,* and surveyed what she had created. One hundred and sixteen boxes and circular shapes, some stacked, some free-standing—all either filled or covered with wood fragments, and all painted black—surrounded her. They had become her world. She knew then that her childhood dream had come true. She was her father's daughter. She had become a sculptor, a builder, an "architect of shadow." She was building *her* empire.

Slowly then, majestically, as the gallery staff watched spellbound, Louise "stripped herself of her workshirt, and radiant with joy . . . started to dance." She was saying "thank you" in her own way to whatever "forces . . . (had) let her achieve her ultimate aim in life: Creation."[14]

Now museums and collectors began to clamor for her work. Louise Nevelson was a recognized artist. She was fifty-eight years old.

* The *one* refers to the viewer.

·N·I·N·E·

"Queen of the Black Black"

LOUISE discovered that she wasn't able to deal with her newfound recognition. She still held on to some of that old anger—the anger that had sustained her for so many desperate years when nothing sold. So when Colette Roberts brought James Sweeney, Director of the Guggenheim Museum, to her studio in the hope of interesting him in buying some of Louise's work for the museum, Louise misinterpreted Sweeney's silence as he surveyed her work. She was certain he simply didn't like it. She escorted him to the garden behind her house and rudely told him, "Look, there's Grand Central Station and behind the Empire State Building is Penn Station. From these two places you can go anywhere in the world. Good day."

On another occasion she snapped at a museum director who apologized for being ten minutes late, "What's ten minutes? Where were you ten years ago?"[1]

THE NEXT YEAR the Martha Jackson Gallery, one of the most prestigious and best financed art galleries in the country, became her representative. They gave Louise a contract that guaranteed her a yearly income. This was the first time since she had left Charles in 1931 that she could relax in the knowledge that she had a steady source of income.

Her first exhibit at Martha Jackson's was *Sky Columns Presence*. As the title implies, these were columns rather than walls. But they were exhibited against the wall, almost like a wall made of columns. (All of Louise's wood sculptures were made to be viewed from the front only.) One piece stood by itself in the center of the room—but the people who came to see it and who called it the *pièce de résistance* would have been surprised—and amused—if they knew how it had come into being.

Louise had worked and worked on a particular box, but she just couldn't get it right. The harder she tried, the worse it seemed. Finally, in a burst of frustration and anger she took a gallon of black paint and *threw* it on the floor. Then she picked up a circular piece she had been working on and jammed it into the box. She *knew* she had it. She called it *The Sun*.[2]

As in the past, all was painted black.

NEAR THE END of 1958, Louise finally accepted the fact that she would have to give up her house on Thirtieth Street. All around her the houses had been vacated, and equipment was being brought in to level the entire area.

It was a difficult time for Louise. This was the first house she had owned—the first that was truly *hers*. More than just a shelter, it had become for her a symbol of security that she didn't want to let go.

Reluctantly, she moved to a house she found in lower Manhattan, a nineteenth-century red brick building at 29 Spring Street. She had the floors stained dark and most of the walls painted black and began to fill the house with neatly separated stacks of her special tools—her wood vocabulary: Renaissance cabinet legs, ornate moldings, fragments of lumber with delicate edges, or machine-cut ones that formed geometric patterns, finials, lintels, a heavy old wooden bannister discarded by a nearby school, "a chaotic army of rejected pieces of wood await(ing) . . . (new) life through a bath of black paint."[3]

In response to questions about her use of black, Louise had often suggested to students, "Try something. Go to Woolworth's and buy something for ten cents and paint it black and you'll see what happens to it." Black had become for her "the total color," "the most aristocratic color of all." "It says more for me than anything else," she would explain. "You can be quiet and it contains the whole thing. There is no color that will give you this feeling of totality. Of peace. Of greatness. Of quietness. Of excitement."[4] It had become her trademark—the dark, the dusk.[5]

QUEEN OF THE BLACK BLACK

Queen of the black black
In the valley of all all
With one glance sees the King.
Mountain top

The Climb
The Way
Restless Winds
Midnight blooms
Tons of colors
Tones of waterdrops
Crystal reflections
Painting mirages.
Celestial splendor.
Highest grandeur
Queen of the black black.
King of the all all[6]

Louise Nelson
1961

What happened next, then, was all the more dramatic and startling. Just as Louise was settling into the house on Spring Street, her friend Dorothy Miller, curator of painting and sculptor at the Museum of Modern Art, phoned and invited her to dinner. When Louise arrived, she was not prepared for what took place. Dorothy asked Louise to participate in the show *Sixteen Americans* at the Museum. Louise was so stunned by the invitation that she impulsively replied, "I'll do a white show." Then she added, "Keep it secret. I want it to be a surprise."[7]

She would be in the Museum of Modern Art! She could hardly believe it. It was the fulfillment of a lifetime dream. It would be "a marriage with the world." She would call it *"Dawn's Wedding Feast.*[8] White would "permit a little something to enter. I don't know whether it's a mood . . . probably a little more light. . . . The white was more festive."[9]

Sixteen Americans was one of a series of American group exhibitions that was presented periodically at the MOMA. Its aim was to bring together distinct and widely varying artists. They would be presented simply as individuals and Americans, but as interesting and exciting contributors to the 1959 American art scene. And Louise would be one of them!

She got to work immediately, planning her exhibit. First, she rented a separate studio nearby to work on the white pieces. She had the walls painted white. "I don't want to be confused," she explained her need for the white studio. And no one but Dorothy must know what she was doing. Her excitement and her energy were at the bursting point. She worked feverishly with only her young assistant Teddy Hazeltine—who had recently come to work for her to help her—completing the entire assemblage in just three months.

As she stood by late in the afternoon of December 16, directing the placement of the splendid, snowy white pieces in what was the largest room in the exhibition at MOMA, watching the creations of her hands and her mind move in to redefine the space, to create ". . . a sense that a whole environment has succumbed to an artist's iron will and velvet eyes,"[10] the tears rolled unheeded down her cheeks as she thought, "If only my mother could have seen this."

With her use of white she had recreated in the stillness of dawn . . . "A gay fantasy . . . resplendent as all Nevelson's dream places are. . ."[11]

Dawn's Wedding Feast—*a fantasy in white, Nevelson's "marriage with the world."* MUSEUM OF MODERN ART.

·T·E·N·

Free to Be a Sensation

LOUISE WENT on to produce an incredibly large body of work and to win acclaim both in the United States and throughout the world.

But she could never remain static. Within two years after the success of her white show she felt the need for something very different from black and more intense than white. As she thought back to the exhibit of Japanese Noh robes at the Metropolitan Museum of Art that had moved her to tears so many years ago, she decided that gold would be the answer.

When she did *Royal Tides*, in 1961, she boldly painted everything gold, imparting a shimmering, jewel-like quality to the boxes. By now she could afford to have her boxes made to order for her, so she was able to "develop a *grid* system of stacking same-size units."[1] When they were sprayed with a muted gold they glowed like a medieval shield. Viewers didn't realize that some of the round forms in the boxes had orginally been toilet seats.

"... *gold comes out of the earth. It's like the sun, it's like the moon—gold." Here, toilet seats are camouflaged by a coat of gold paint.* **Royal Tide II,** *1961–63, painted wood.* PHOTOGRAPH BY GEOFFREY CLEMENTS, WHITNEY MUSEUM OF AMERICAN ART, GIFT OF THE ARTIST.

Gold came after white. ". . . gold comes out of the earth. It's like the sun, it's like the moon—gold. There's more gold in nature than we give credit for, because every day there are certain reflections where the sun's rays hit and you get gold."[2] But it was her new secure financial situation that allowed her to say, "Gold is the sun glinting, but it is CASH. Gold is money in the bank."[3]

The next year Louise was selected by the Museum of Modern Art to represent the United States at the prestigious *XXXI Biennale Internazionale d'Arte, Venezia*, the oldest and most famous of the international art shows. She created three environments—one black, one white, one gold—for the three rooms in the United States Pavilion. Each room would become a world of its own.

Louise and Dorothy Miller flew to Venice together via London. As occasionally happens in such situations, while the two women changed planes in London, one of Louise's bags did not.

When they debarked in Venice they found that Louise's luggage had not arrived. All her clothes for the opening night reception and subsequent parties, her Chinese robes, were in the missing bag. She *had* to have that bag.

When she asked how long it would take to locate it, the unperturbed official calmly responded, "Oh, maybe in a few days. . . " This was Saturday evening. The exhibition would open on Monday.

Louise knew she had to do something. She looked him square in the eye and said, "Now, I'm getting married tomorrow and I've got to have my trousseau. My white wedding dress is in it." (Louise was sixty-two years old.) The officials got so nervous they made some phone calls, sent a wire—and the bag appeared in Venice on Sunday.[4]

Within a short time after the exhibit opened to the public, everyone in Venice was calling this World's Fair of Art "Louise Nevelson's Show." But few people in her hometown of Rockland, Maine, even knew of her work.

———————————————

BY THIS TIME Louise had already established her uniquely personal style of dress. Fashion had always been an important part of her life. She had loved large hats, beautiful clothes, wonderful jewelry since she had been a young girl. Now she decided, "I'm constantly creating. Why should I stop with myself?"

She had always been daring—in her life, in her art— and she had always had a flair for fashion. Now she was becoming even more daring in her selection of clothes. "Let's break tradition there, too," she thought. Her statement would be *collage*. After all, her art was collage. "I love to put things together. My whole life is one big collage. Every time I put on clothes I am creating a picture."[5] She even talks like a collage: "I don't like to finish sentences." She has been described as a "collage driven relentlessly to excess, a cross between Catherine the Great and a bag lady."[6]

Her love of theater, her sense of the dramatic, her recollections of her mother, and later, of Princess Norina Matchabelli and Martha Graham all came into play here. So this tall, graceful, striking woman began to combine disparate garments into an ensemble that would work for her. She would pull together different fabrics, textures, colors, assembling them into a whole that made a dramatic statement. "I love being a lady and dressing up and masquerading and wearing all the fineries."[7]

And she began to wear false eyelashes—several pairs of enormous, thick, mink lashes glued together. These would become her trademark. She doesn't feel dressed without them. She wears no other makeup on her smooth skin. Indeed, it has been said, "Mrs. N's eyelashes come into the room before she does." But it is these eyelashes together with the invariable long skirts and bandana on her head that make her instantly recognizable.

It is as likely that Louise Nevelson will wear a sixteenth-century Mandarin Chinese robe over a blue denim workshirt, as a Scaasi-designed gown of embroidered Indian silk with a brown jockey cap. "I've always felt free to be a sensation," she has said. But perhaps her appearance is deceptive. "If you're going to put on a show like I do, they don't know beneath that facade there's something else."[8]

She mixes different kinds of fabrics from many different cultures—Chinese, Mexican, Persian, Pennsylvania Dutch, Egyptian. And she wears what she feels like wearing, when she feels like wearing it. The same assemblage of clothes might go to work, then to dinner, and on to sleep!

Louise had learned as a little girl—when she was transplanted from Russia to Rockland—how to be different.

———————

AT THE CONCLUSION of the Venice Biennale Louise appeared to be riding high. Her art was being exhibited—and acclaimed—around the world. Sidney Janis, director of the most important gallery in New York at the time, invited her to be the first woman and the first American sculptor ever to have a one-woman show at his gallery. And she was elected president of Artists Equity, the largest organization of professional painters, sculptors and graphic artists in the United States.

But things weren't quite what they seemed. Her gallery relationships were deteriorating. (Daniel Cordier was exhibiting her work in his galleries in Paris and Frankfurt now, and Martha Jackson was her representative in New York.) Louise found that she couldn't meet the demands of the two art dealers. Yet her decision to leave both of them to join the Janis Gallery was an even greater mistake. The arrangement with Sidney Janis seems to have been a failure almost before it began. Perhaps their personalities didn't mesh, perhaps the financial arrangement was not ideal for Louise—perhaps both. But her work didn't sell, and she wasn't able to repay the money she had borrowed in order to prepare the show. (While her work was acclaimed artistically, people still were not ready to invest large sums of money in "old wood" to place in their fashionably decorated homes.) The spring of 1963 found her once again in debt, disappointed and depressed.[9]

A totally unexpected invitation saved her. She was offered a two-month fellowship by the Tamarind Lithography Workshop under a Ford Foundation grant to experiment with new techniques in printmaking at their campus in Los Angeles. This was the perfect opportunity for her to escape the gray winter of New York and exchange it for the warmth and sunshine of California. All her expenses would be paid.

Once again, at Tamarind, as she had ten years before at Atelier 17, she shunned the conventional tools of the craft and used her own materials to get the image she wanted. In so doing Louise expanded the medium, bringing originality and a breath of fresh air to the traditional print forms.

She had a large paper bag filled with crocheted doilies, pieces of gauze and netting, even rags. These she would cut into different shapes and sizes, then place them on a stone, layer upon layer, until they produced a three-dimensional effect. Here again her collage aesthetic was at work. She would arrange and rearrange the forms—until she had created the design she wanted. This would be printed on lovely hand-made paper. In spite of her loneliness, she loved the work.

The designs Louise produced at Tamarind seem to transmit the feel of the shadows cast by the trees that surrounded her as she worked. "If these had been done in New York," she said, "there would have been more evidence of buildings."[10]

Tamarind had the desired effect on Louise. When June Wayne, director of the workshop, told her that no artist had ever produced as many prints as she in six weeks, her spirits soared. She returned to New York refreshed, regenerated, and ready to build more walls. She joined the new Pace Gallery, a relationship that she maintains today. Pace, under the direction of Arnold Glimcher, has grown over the years to become one of the most prestigious galleries in New York—and in the country. (It is located very near the space occupied by Karl Nierendorf in the 1940s.)

Fired with enthusiasm, she composed *Homage 6,000,000 I*, a huge black wall (eighteen feet across and nine feet high) overflowing with geometric shapes—rectangles, triangles, circles—furniture parts and giant yarn spools.

Louise was on her way. And she had returned to black, to what she loved the best—the dark, the dusk. "For me—my own feeling—I go back to black."[11]

By the time, two years later, that the Israel Museum opened on a stony Judean hill in Jerusalem, Louise had completed *Homage 6,000,000 II*, her tribute to "a people who have triumphed." Commemorating the victims of Nazi terror, it was called "a modern-day book of the dead, but also triumphantly a book of life . . . looking to the future while not forgetting the past."[12] She presented it to the museum as her gift in 1966.

The poem accompanying Homage 6,000,000 II, *found among the Nevelson papers, revealed the depth of her feeling. (overleaf)*

One lives a life
The layers of consciousness are infinite
My own awareness is my own awareness

The essence and symbols of this presence will be a living presence of a people who have triumphed.

They rose far and above the greatest that was inflicted upon them.

I hear all over this earth a livingness and a presence of these peoples.

I feel they are here, and there is a song I hear and that song that rings in my ears and that song is here. We will give homes all over this earth. And that song will live on, that song is in every crevice of livingness.

The depth of what I feel must remain private. I cannot speak of it out loud. Their consciousness and our consciousness are one.

reflection—exaltation—six million equals epic grandeur

In the millions of corners of this earth millions of reflections, and these reflections are the most livingness and the livingness it is all here, and we will be with them side by side for ever and forever.

Time is standing still for us in this presence

They have given us a livingness.

Louise Nevelson—1965

*Commemorating the victims of Nazi terror, this is
Louise Nevelson's tribute "to a people who have triumphed."*
Homage 6,000,000 II, *1964, painted wood.*
ISRAEL MUSEUM, JERUSALEM, GIFT OF THE ARTIST
THROUGH THE AMERICAN ISRAEL CULTURAL FOUNDATION.

Adding~ New Dimensions

LOUISE'S constantly restless mind began searching for other modes of expression. She was ready for new materials. She moved easily into plexiglass and aluminum, which was lightweight and flexible. "I didn't even have to cross the room."

Then, after the new building of the Whitney Museum opened officially on September 27, 1966, the museum mounted the first retrospective exhibit of her work. On March 8, 1967, shortly after the conclusion of an exhibition of the paintings of Andrew Wyeth, the entire fourth floor of the building became a showcase for her work—a Nevelson *environment*. It included not only many of her wood pieces done over the years, but went back to her early terra cotta figures and up to her newest clear plexiglass sculpture, a small piece (only twenty-four inches by twenty-six inches by twelve inches) entitled *Ice Palace*.

Arnold Glimcher tells a revealing story about the retrospective. Two days before the scheduled opening he went to the museum with Louise for a last minute check of the installation. She was happy with the placement of the pieces and with the lighting. Then she came upon a large black plaster figure of a woman, called *Earth Figure*, that had been made many years before. Louise had never liked this piece and did not want to exhibit it. But curator John Gordon of the museum had prevailed upon her to include it in the interest of making the exhibition complete.

Impulsively, Louise asked her friend to pick up the sculpture and carry it to the other side of the room. He complied. Suddenly, she shouted, "Drop it!" Startled, he let go, and *Earth Figure* smashed to bits.

Louise immediately phoned John Gordon, told him there had been an accident, and assured him that it was completely her fault. "She was now satisfied with the exhibition; she had edited out the weakest piece."[1]

LOUISE was in her seventies when she began doing monumental outdoor sculpture in Cor-Ten steel.* "Now something in the living conscious being has a beat, and you move on."[2] She was ready now to "take away the enclosures and come out into the open and let the out-of-doors be the reflection."[3]

She was ready, too, for the new material. She found herself "using steel as if it were ribbon made out of satin."[4] A new dimension had been added to her work.

But now, because of the size and the weight of the material she could no longer compose spontaneously herself. Occasionally it became necessary for her to make small cardboard models—sculptural sketches—of her ideas that the workers at the Lippincott Foundry in North

* a type of steel that oxidizes to a rusty color on the surface only, thereby forming a protective coating that prevents deterioration.

Haven, Connecticut, would, in a leap of faith, transpose into reality. This was something she had never done for her wooden assemblages.

When she tried to use wood as a maquette (model) for the metal, she found that it didn't work. The texture, the weight, the scale were not the same. The wood and the metal had to be treated differently.

Lippincott, the foremost fabricator of massive sculpture in the East, quickly became her "sculpture factory," the place where art and technology could come together. Soon she became the only sculptor to work with the men at the foundry. She was able to convey her ideas to them, then watch them spot-weld the materials. Then, if she didn't like the effect—if the relationship between the pieces didn't please her—it was easy to change. She set a hectic pace for the men there. Whether she was finding metal scraps on the floor or explaining her specific requirements for custom cut and shaped pieces, her great energy quickly became contagious.

Working at the foundry one day, she was dressed in a long paisley skirt with a blue denim work shirt and an Indian vest, topped by a plaid woolen lumberjack shirt. To this she had added a red leather belt hung around her neck as a necklace, and had wrapped the invariable kerchief around her head, almost as a queen might wear a crown. Then, her beautiful face devoid of makeup save for the incredible eyelashes, and with gilded space sandals on her feet, she moved with the agility and assuredness of a very young woman, politely telling the men who were moving pieces into place for her: "I would make it an inch lower. You know, that could be another inch—is that going to be awfully hard to do? Now let's put it a little higher and see what would happen. I think that's the way it has to be. I

think that's the way it *will* be." She was a gentle but determined perfectionist whose creative energy, even in her seventies, had not waned. The love for what she was doing
seemed to take the weight out of the work. "Physical activity can be a great source of intelligence," she has said.

Her first commissioned large-scale Cor-Ten steel
sculpture was for Princeton University. Many others followed across the country from Massachusetts Institute of
Technology in Cambridge, Massachusetts, to the Embar-
cadero Center in San Francisco, California.

In December of 1972, as her great gift to New York,
the city she loves, the city she refers to as one "great big
sculpture," and "the great collage of our universe," she
completed a twenty-two-and-a-half-foot-high sculpture of
Cor-Ten steel. *Night Presence IV* was installed at the entrance to Central Park at Fifth Avenue and Sixtieth Street.
(It would later be moved to a permanent location on Park
Avenue at Ninety-second Street.)

Wrapped in an ankle-length chinchilla coat and wearing a brown jockey cap against the chill winter winds,
Louise told those assembled for the occasion that it was her
Christmas gift "to this wonderful city where I have lived
and worked and created for fifty years." She concluded,
". . . I thought it fitting I should give it something of myself."[5]

The city would honor her in return six years later by
naming a half-block-long triangle in lower Manhattan
Louise Nevelson Plaza, and installing seven huge welded
steel sculptures, *Shadows and Flags*, there. Before she
began to design the sculptures, Louise went to the top of
several of the towering buildings in the financial district
that surround the tiny park to view the area from that
perspective. Then she decided to put the sculptures on legs

so they would appear to "float like flags."[6]

One year later, at two o'clock in the afternoon of November 11, 1973, residents of the lovely little desert town of Scottsdale, Arizona, flocked to its Civic Center Plaza to join in the celebration of the unveiling of Louise's monumental sculpture, *Windows to the West*. In a ceremony typical of many others held in major cities across the country over the years, those gathered watched dancing, heard music by Aaron Copland, and listened to Louise Nevelson describe the fifteen-foot Cor-Ten steel structure:

> We look through the inside mass to see a multitude of paintings and photographs: the mountains, the trees, the skies of Arizona.

Then, just one month later, on Sunday afternoon, December 16, in what must have been a significant moment, Louise spoke from the pulpit of Temple Israel in Boston. It was a celebration of the unveiling of *Sky Covenant* adjacent to the front door of that institution. It had been the rabbi of Temple Israel who had performed the ceremony when Louise Berliawsky married Charles Nevelson fifty-three years before.

THROUGH IT ALL, while she continued to design monumental steel sculptures, Louise never abandoned wood.

> Different people have different memories . . .
> mine happens to be for form. Basically, my memory is for wood, which gives a certain kind of form.[7]

She liked the textures of the wood, and what she has always referred to as its *livingness*.

"*We look through the inside mass to see a multitude of paintings and photographs: the mountains, the trees, the skies of Arizona.*"
Atmosphere and Environment XIII (*Windows to the West*), 1972. *Cor-Ten steel, Scottsdale, Arizona.* PHOTOGRAPH BY L. H. BOBER.

I like it that life twisted those old nails and wood.
I also like it that in back of them you still see a
human hand.[8]

The poorest, the cheapest woods can be the most exciting
to her. Often they have a history and a drama long forgotten. Her joy is in bringing them back to life and transform-
ing them into something beautiful.

Art is everywhere, except it has to pass through a
creative mind.[9]

One time, when she decided that she needed bent
wood for a composition, she put some wood into a bathtub
full of water to see what would happen. She was always
quick to try something *before* she looked for information
about it. "That's why I produce so much. Usually you can
make things work."[10]

She uses the cracks in the old wood where the nails
have come out as drawings. "I'm drawing all the time," she
has said. "When I put pieces together . . . I'm applying
drawing as well. It seems I make all my work *just to
draw.*"[11]

Take two fingers and you will see a line between
them. Well, that's what gives these two fingers
their definition . . . and that's just what makes my
work. It's really the line between two objects.[12]

———————————

BUT THE "house" was still not complete. Her limitless
reaching out to new forms and new materials continued.

Accomplishment in each medium—old wood, plexiglass, aluminum, steel, etchings, lithographs—seemed to fuel her never-ending need to create on still other levels. So it was that customers in Macy's Department Store were startled one day to see this elegant, majestic lady in her multi-layered assemblage of clothes, but with comfortable space-sandals on her feet, ride the escalator up to the toy department and order Playschool blocks and Lincoln logs by the hundreds. Their precise, geometric forms and their smooth surfaces—in stark contrast to the ragged edges and rough textures of the *found* wood—would add yet another dimension to her work.

> The world is unlimited. The artist must never limit himself.[13]

When she begins composing, the pieces are there, sorted according to shape, size, texture. This is her stock, her raw material. Some of the wood may have been waiting for years to be used. Like a wood witch casting a spell, she uses these fragments of another time to create totally new images with the mysterious and moving power of poetry.

> Sometimes it's the material that takes over; sometimes it's me . . . I permit them to play, like a seesaw. I use action and counteraction, like in music. . . . It was always a relationship—my speaking to the wood, and the wood speaking back to me. . . . I permit it to move to how I feel, how it weighs

Overleaf: "Art is everywhere, except it has to pass through a creative mind." Louise Nevelson's "wood vocabulary."
PHOTOGRAPH BY AL MOZELL, THE PACE GALLERY.

and how it moves. . . . my feeling and the sculpture become one. It's a love affair, and it becomes
one.[14]

This is the *oneness* she had dreamed about so many
years before.

The work you do every day . . . and you are one,
the work is a living example, it's just as living as
you are. It's your reflection.[15]

Nothing else matters. "I leave the world to the world. I just
do my thing."[16] She had decided when she was very young
that art, for her, would be a solitary venture, a place to live
and breathe in. She knew she would have to go her own
way. She had no choice. The kind of life she wanted for
herself didn't permit her to make compromises, or to have
compartments in her head. It had to be clear. "I had to
have totality day and night."

Often when she went to sleep at night the forms she
was working on would move around in her head as though
they were people.

Now if I had a mate at that time there would have
been intrusions—maybe delightful, but they
would have been intrusions nevertheless.
Whereas this way, good or not, it was a totality
. . . I needed it.[17]

"I am closer to the work than to anything on earth. That's
the marriage." She has compared intrusions on the mind
to splinters: "If you have one small splinter in it [your hand]
you can't function."[18]

She loves being with people when she's not working: "I don't always have time, but somehow we can try to accommodate ourselves—to have some fun. I call on fun. It's a *must!*"[19] Yet she has lived alone for most of her adult life. She has been completely alone for decision-making. "That's the price you pay for freedom."[20]

This need to go her own way extended to her art as well. She never belonged to any movement in art: "Artists reflect their time, but they have to stand on their own two feet."[21] She could absorb all the influences around her, then go on to evolve a style of her own.

———————————————

GENERALLY, Louise gets up at 6:00 A.M. and works until she is physically exhausted. Every evening she puts her tools away, sweeps her studio (even this is done rhythmically, beautifully) and lays out the things she wants for the following morning. In this way she can begin to work as soon as she wakes up. "Everything is clean, nice."[22]

But she objects to the word *work*. "I think *work* is a bad word, because *work* means labor and this is not labor."[23]

"In my studio I'm as happy as a cow in a stall. That's the only place where everything is all right."[24]

The Search Continues

LOUISE has gone on to receive many accolades, and to produce an incredibly large body of work. In 1975, she completed her largest wood sculpture to date, *Bicentennial Dawn*, commissioned for the James A. Byrne Federal Courthouse in Philadelphia. It was described by art critic Emily Genauer as the most beautiful public sculpture anywhere in the country.[1]

In what may well be considered the climax of her work, Louise built a very personal environment at the Pace Gallery just two years later—an actual room into which the viewer could enter, at the same time entering, for a moment perhaps, into the magical world of Louise Nevelson. Drawing on the affectionate name that the children in her neighborhood call her, Louise titled the work *Mrs. N's Palace*. This seemed to be the culmination of a project that she had begun fihe had made a series of "dream houses -made doll houses to which she had attached her compions of geometric shapes.

Mrs. N's Palace was a wide but shallow room in which black wood reliefs lined the walls, hung from the ceiling and stood in groups on a black mirror floor. Two figures, a king and a queen constructed many years before, stood just inside the entrance.

Only three blocks downtown from the Pace Gallery, in the newly completed Citicorp Building, a soaring sky-scraper on Lexington Avenue, at the same time that Mrs. N's Palace was on exhibition, Louise once again brilliantly broke tradition. She became the first American artist to completely design a chapel in the United States. The sculptures that suggest grapes and grain, the Trinity and the Apostles, the striking white and gold crucifix, the benches for meditation, even the priests' vestments, were all designed by Louise Nevelson. In the Chapel of the Good Shepherd in St. Peter's Lutheran Church she showed once again her tremendous versatility. The darkness, the magic, the confines of Mrs. N's Palace opened up here to the almost blindingly beautiful all-white chapel, an oasis of calm within the huge and bustling Citicorp Center.

The tiny chapel, an oddly shaped five-sided room, seats only twenty-eight people in pews set herringbone fashion, instead of facing the altar. Each wall holds a typical Nevelson sculpture that manages to strike a delicate balance between religion and art.

At the cornerstone ceremony, held across the street at Central Synagogue, where Lutheran Church services had been held during the two years that St. Peter's Church was being rebuilt, Louise reminisced that one of her uncles had won a competition and designed "a blue ceiling with stars in it"[2] for a government church in Russia many many years before. She told those assembled: "We've broken barriers on both sides with this and we hope to break more." It was her "gift to the Universe."

Why had a Russian-born Jewish artist been selected to design a Lutheran chapel in New York? the pastor of St. Peter's was asked. "Because she's the greatest living American sculptor," was his reply.[3]

OVER THE YEARS, colleges all across the country have honored her by conferring honorary degrees. Brandeis University gave her their coveted Creative Arts Award in 1971. She was invited to dinner at the White House by President and Mrs. Gerald Ford in 1974, and was one of five women artists honored there in 1979, when Jimmy Carter was President. She was also elected to membership in the American Academy of Arts and Letters that year. Two sections from *Dawn's Wedding Feast* were installed in the main reception hall of the Governor's Mansion in Albany when Nelson Rockefeller was Governor of New York.

She—and her work—have traveled all over the world, including a foray to Japan, but it is likely that no trip has given her as much pleasure as the one she made back to Rockland in 1979. It was with particular pride and joy that she could return to this town that had seemed so alien to her as she was growing up and find herself the *star* she used to dream of being when she was a little girl there—to find herself feted and honored and sought after, and, in fact, treated like the queen she had wanted to become—indeed *had* become. She was eighty years old and Rockland was making her a birthday party.

In honor of the event the Farnsworth Library and Art

Frieze of the Apostles (east wall) in the Chapel of the Good Shepherd, St. Peter's Church, New York, 1977. An oasis of calm.
PHOTOGRAPH BY L. H. BOBER.

Museum mounted a retrospective of her work—an over-
view of her career that spanned the preceding forty years.
Work had been borrowed from museums and private collections all across the country. As she stood between Nate
and Anita (Lillian had died two years before) at the celebration, she thought how proud her parents would have been
to see her now.

"It's been a fascinating life, hasn't it?" Nate whispered
to her.

"Yes. God, yes. But tough, tough," she answered him.

* * *

WITH ALL her accomplishments, all the bravado and
seeming ego of her personality, one thread has been woven
continuously through the fabric of her life—the giving of
herself and her resources to those less fortunate than she.
No matter how much prominence, professional recognition and acclaim Louise has achieved, she has never lost
touch with her roots. Quietly, with dignity and with gen-
erosity, she has worked with groups whose goals are as
diverse as helping Jews to flee from Russia, supporting the
State of Israel, saving police headquarters in Little Italy,
and cancer research.

"I lead a simple life at home, so I have time for what I
want," she explains it. When asked why she does so much
her immediate retort is, "I want to do it!"[4]

* * *

AND SHE REMAINS a concerned mother. Her brief
notes to Mike reminding him to take his vitamins, or to

take care of his feet no longer surprise him. A visitor to Mike's studio in Connecticut, obsessively neat and filled with his own wooden sculptures, was amused recently to hear him answer the telephone and say, "Yes, Mother. Yes, I've eaten. I *had* lunch. I *have* eaten, Mother."[5]

Her own tastes in food are very simple, and she eats very little—to rid herself of unnecessary decision-making. A visit to her house on Spring Street in Manhattan's Little Italy (where her neighbors call her *La Signora of Spring Street*) reveals an unusually simple—even austere—interior. It has grown from the single building that she originally purchased at Number 29 to include the two on either side of it. One had been a private sanitarium, the other an enormous garage. Dividing walls were torn down and the buildings united so that now there are seventeen rooms, several kitchens and many baths on a series of levels.

"An artist like myself never has enough space." Space, to Louise Nevelson, is more precious than diamonds. "It's asking to be filled."[6]

"Your concept of what you put into a space will create another space. I have seen a person walk in a room and dominate the space."[7] She does just that herself. Her commanding presence is felt immediately. As she sweeps into a room, looks around and quickly says, "I'll sit here," she conveys a sense of royalty. Her movement, her dress, even her speech—soft, distinct, and with the broad *a* of the New Englander—and the excitement she generates are like the constant turning of the colors in a kaleidoscope. Her work may be black (which she insists contains *all* color), but she herself is color personified.

The space in her house is constantly changing. It is no longer the place she moved into in 1958. Light streams in through its forty-seven windows, brightening the highly polished black floors and marble stairs worn thin and concave at the center from years of use. The ceilings and one or two of the walls in each room are painted black, the rest white. Her sculptures are everywhere.

There is no distinction between living space and working space because she has made no distinction between her life and her art. Home to her is a place to work and to exhibit. It is *not* a domestic haven.[8] The rooms contain very little furniture—simple gray metal storage cabinets, formica tables and straight-back chairs. There is no upholstered furniture. "Soft chairs invite boring conversations." Besides, visitors might stay too long!

> I have a way of living that suits me. I'm not pushing to make others comfortable.[9]

Louise has ten desks throughout the house to accommodate all her papers. One, made by Mike, is in the shape of a person. But she likes to sit at the kitchen table to open her mail, using scissors to do this. Ripping anything would offend her sensibilities.

Most of her possessions are out of sight. Nothing must impose itself on her. "Objects have vibrations that intrude." But it has not always been like that.

During the first years that Louise lived on Spring Street she filled the house with her collections—African masks and early American tools were hung on the one brick wall in the living room. Her collections of American Indian

Louise Nevelson on a recent visit to Mexico, a country whose culture has been a continuing source of inspiration to her work.
PHOTOGRAPH BY DIANA MACKOWN.

pottery, pre-Columbian sculptures, African figures and Puerto Rican *santos* were lined up next to one another on a shelf that spanned one wall. The hallways downstairs were hung floor to ceiling with her collection of paintings, and upstairs they were filled with her own early paintings. At one time she owned over one hundred paintings by Eilshemius. She had a great collection of Ralph Rosenborg's paintings, and many other artists' works as well. "For a minute I had a Paul Klee." One had the sense of being in a museum.

By 1966, she had sold most of her possessions and stripped the house to its bare essentials.

Today her bedroom on the fourth floor has been compared to an army barracks. It contains only a bed covered with an Indian blanket, a sculpture done by Mike, and steel lockers to hold her clothing. Scarves are folded, shoe boxes and hat boxes are neatly stacked. Everything is orderly, precise. Fur coats, brocade dresses, Chinese robes and long Scaasi skirts are hung on racks behind a wall of closed doors. The walls in the hallway are bare.[10]

The collections have sprouted again, but this time they are hidden from view. The cupboards contain a wealth of "treasures"—china, crystal, silver, pewter, candlesticks, boxes, trays. It is the *act* of collecting, though, not the fact of ownership that intrigues her.

> The wonder of collecting is that you are constantly in training to look for that added dimension that you identify with.[11]

She loves living with her collections, touching them, cleaning them. When she polishes her silver she sees the forms in the pieces, the designs that were etched on them. She seems to communicate with them and they become a part of her. Later their forms find their way into her own art. Occasionally, as the mood strikes her, she will take a few pieces from their cupboard and arrange them in an exquisite still life, "to please the inner being."[12]

Louise has said that she never consciously wanted to be a collector, ". . . but somehow . . . these things come to me, and before I know it there's a collection."[13]

She comes by this penchant for collecting naturally. "Artists are born collectors," she muses, as she thinks back to her room full of "treasures" in Rockland, and to her father's warehouse full of antiques. Now it even extends to the pieces of wood she collects and sometimes saves for years until she finds exactly the right use for them in her sculpture.

"I collect for my eye," she has said. And she has an exceptional eye. She believes that anyone can live in great beauty anywhere, as long as you're alive to your environment. She loves to tell people that she lives on the Bowery, then watch the expressions on their faces. Even from there, she can "see the world." Sitting in her dining room and looking out at the huge school building that once stood across the street she could find varying patterns in the way the sun and the moon reflected on its windows. She can look at a chair and say, "The chair isn't so hot, but look at its shadow."[14]

Many years ago, in Texas for a brief stopover on her way to California, she was shopping for souvenirs to bring back to her family when she spotted an Indian pot on a shelf. She *had* to have that pot. It had the geometry, the design that she understood. And it was the terra cotta that she loved. But it was not for sale.

Determined, she prevailed upon the owner of the shop until he finally consented to sell it to her. Then, fearful that it might get lost or broken, she refused to have it shipped home. Instead, she wrapped it in paper, then put it in a basket, placed the basket into a carton, and carried the whole from city to city herself until she returned to New York. So began her collection of Indian pottery.[15]

Whenever Louise travels she haunts the antique shops in the area, searching for treasure. Recently she flew to Chicago for the opening of an exhibition of her work. Before the start of the evening's festivities she paid a visit to her favorite antique dealer just outside the city. As she entered his shop she saw hanging off to the side a very old fringed *Dashiki*, a loose-fitting shirt of coarse woven fabric covered with bits of mirror and pieces of wood, all symbols of an ancient African culture. She bought it immediately, then gaily wore it to the party that night—over the black lace blouse she had brought along for the occasion.[16] Perhaps this is one of the reasons that she was named to the *Best Dressed* list in 1977: "There was nowhere else to put her and no way to ignore her."[17]

EARLY IN 1983, when Louise Nevelson was eighty-three years old, she had an exhibition at the Pace Gallery of work done over the previous three years. Entitled *Cascades, Perpendiculars, Silence, Music*, the all-black wood pieces were composed from remnants of an organ that had been damaged by a fire in 1978 at the Church of St. Mark near her home. Once again, pieces of former beauty and usefulness, with a past of their own, had been taken apart, bathed in black paint, and given new life as they were reassembled into a totally different setting. Exhibited in an *environment* through which the viewer could wander in muted light that gave them an almost nocturnal quality, they proved that her powerful poetic vision was still intact. One review of the exhibition said:

> If any female artist has earned an evaluation without reference to gender, Mrs. Nevelson would certainly seem to be the one. . . . Her reinterpretation and original expression of a female sensibility in such a nontraditional body of work challenges our most fundamental stereotypes.[18]

The review pointed up once again how Louise Nevelson has broken tradition. Long before the advent of "women's liberation" she competed successfully in an area that had always been dominated by men. She was so absorbed in what she was doing, and so certain of her own ability that it had never occurred to her that being a woman might be a handicap.

She has always considered her work delicate, feminine. "True strength is delicate." She has never used the tools a man uses—but often will cut wood with a scissor. "A man wouldn't do that."[19]

She had long ago made the choice to dedicate her life to art. She had the courage to make that choice. The strength came from her belief in herself. She knew what she had. She made it a reality. She could go beyond the frontier.

WHILE THE EXHIBIT at the Pace Gallery was going on, a retrospective of her work was mounted at the Nassau County Museum of Fine Art in Roslyn Harbor, Long Island. Speaking to a group of people there Louise reminisced that she had been searching for an *ultimate* since she was very young, but had been unable to find it. In her mid-seventies, she said, as she looked back on all her work, she decided that there shouldn't be an *ultimate*. Her answer would be a *question mark*.

She thought back to her father's adherence to the teachings of the *Talmud* and realized that, in effect, her work was a living example. She knew that somewhere in her inner being she, like her father, was a builder. She had built an empire. But it was "an empire of aesthetics, and that is the true empire for me, and it's never limited and *you never finish*. It is a personal empire of recognition."[20] She would leave something open.

My total conscious search in life has been for a new seeing, a new image, a new insight.[21]

The search continues. The house remains unfinished.

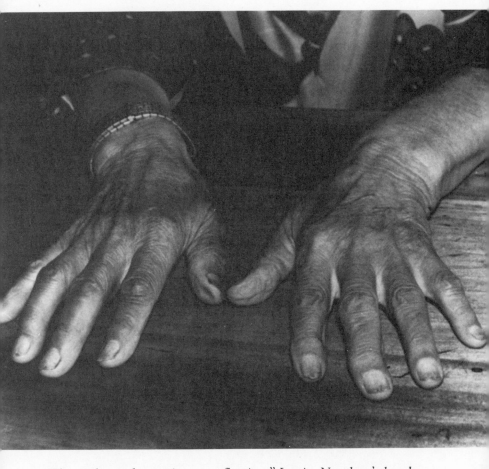

"The work you do . . . is your reflection." Louise Nevelson's hands.
PHOTOGRAPH BY DIANA MACKOWN.

Chapter Notes

Chapter One   **Jars of Colored Candy**

1. *World of Our Fathers*. Irving Howe. p. 10.
2. Interview with Louise Nevelson, July 29, 1982.
3. Ibid.
4. *Dawns + Dusks*. Diana MacKown. p. 6.
5. Ibid., p. 9.
6. Interview with Anita Weinstein, Rockland, Maine, March 23, 1982.
7. Ibid.
8. Louise Nevelson: Talk at Cooper Union, November 22, 1982.
9. *Dawns + Dusks*, p. 14.

Chapter Two   **Gathering Treasures**

1. Interview with Anita Weinstein, March 23, 1982.
2. Telephone interview with Louise Nevelson, April 13, 1983.
3. *Dawns + Dusks*, p. 25.
4. Ibid., p. 24.
5. Interview with Anita Weinstein, March 23, 1982.
6. Ibid.
7. *Dawns + Dusks*, p. 10.
8. *Louise Nevelson: Iconography and Source*. Laurie Wilson. p. 48.
9. Ibid., p. 51.
10. *Dawns + Dusks*, p. 25.
11. Interview with Anita Weinstein, March 23, 1982.

Chapter Three   Trapped in the "Promised Land"

1. *The City of New York*. Jerry Patterson. p. 217.

Chapter Four   Search for an Anchor

1. "Debacle of the Modern Theatre," by Friederich Kiesler, pp. 14–24 (in program of International Theatre Exposition)
2. *Dawns + Dusks*, p. 38.
3. *Max Reinhardt and His Theatre*. Oliver M. Sayler, ed.
4. *Dawns + Dusks*, p. 31.
5. Ibid., p. 37.
6. *Iconography and Source*, pp. 61–62.
7. Conversation with Louise Nevelson, February 20, 1983.
8. *Dawns + Dusks*, p. 40.
9. Ibid., p. 43.
10. Ibid., p. 46.

Chapter Five   Dance to Freedom

1. *Dawns + Dusks*, pp. 43–44.
2. Letter to Louise Nevelson from Mike (no date), Archives of American Art.
3. Ibid., Winter, 1931–2.
4. Ibid., Spring, 1932.
5. Ibid., February 2, 1932.
6. *Dawns + Dusks*, p. 46.
7. Quoted by Arnold Glimcher, in *Louise Nevelson*, p. 38.
8. *Dawns + Dusks*, p. 57.
9. Glimcher, op. cit., p. 41.

10. Ibid., p. 42.

11. *Dawns + Dusks*, p. 65.

12. Ibid., p. 57.

13. Interview with Louise Nevelson, July 29, 1982.

14. Edwin Denby, *Looking At Dance.* p. 407.

15. *Dawns + Dusks*, p. 67.

16. Ibid., pp. 65–66.

17. Wilson, op. cit., p. 70.

Chapter Six   "I *Am* A Woman's Liberation"

1. *Art and Life in America.* Oliver W. Larkin. p. 409.

2. *Flatbush.* June, 1935, p. 3. (Louise Nevelson)

3. Wilson, op. cit., p. 73.

4. *Independents of the Twentieth Century.* Constance Schwartz. p. 9.

5. *Dawns + Dusks*, p. 59.

6. Letter dated January 13, 1953, Archives of American Art.

7. *Dawns + Dusks*, p. 73.

8. R. Bongartz. *New York Times Magazine,* January 24, 1971, p. 33.

9. *Dawns + Dusks*, pp. 69–70.

10. *Art Talk.* Cindy Nemser. pp. 60–61.

11. Letter dated January 24, 1934, Archives of American Art.

12. Glimcher, op. cit., p. 47.

13. *Dawns + Dusks*, pp. 75–76.

14. *Cue*, October 4, 1941, p. 16.

15. *New York Times*, September 28, 1941.

16. *New York Herald Tribune*, September 28, 1941.

17. *New York World Telegram*, September 27, 1941. (Emily Genauer)

18. *Dawns + Dusks*, p. 76.

19. Letter dated October 9, 1941, Archives of American Art.

20. *Dawns + Dusks*, p. 94.

21. Ibid., p. 76.

22. Ibid.

Chapter Seven   **"A World of Geometry and Magic"**

1. *Dawns + Dusks*, p. 90.

2. *Out of this Century*. Peggy Guggenheim. p. 246.

3. Wilson, op. cit., p. 121.

4. *Arts*, February, 1959, p. 51. (Hilton Kramer)

5. *Dawns + Dusks*, p. 92.

6. *Corriere D'America*, January 10, 1943. (Lou Nappi)

7. Letter to Louise Nevelson from Joe Milone dated November 14, 1942, Archives of American Art.

8. *Dawns + Dusks*, p. 93.

9. *New York Times*, February 3, 1943.

10. *Fourth Dimension*. Laurie Wilson. p. 14.

11. *Cue*, November 13, 1948, p. 18.

12. *Dawns + Dusks*, p. 94.

13. Interview with Louise Nevelson, July 29, 1982.

14. Letter dated June 20, 1943, Archives of American Art.

15. Letter from Peggy Guggenheim dated May 26, 1946, Archives of American Art.

16. Quoted by Wilson in *Iconography and Source*, p. 127.

17. On view at the Museum of Fine Art, Roslyn, New York, January 20–April 10, 1983.

18. *Dawns + Dusks*, p. 102.

19. Ibid., p. 105.

20. Quoted by Laurie Wilson, *Iconography and Source*, p. 84.

21. *Dawns + Dusks*, p. 107.

22. *Nevelson*. Pace Catalogue, 1974. (Introduction by Louise Nevelson)

23. *History of Art for Young People*. H. W. Jansen. p. 254.

Chapter Eight   Boxes and Compartments:
Jars of Colored Candy Remembered

1. *Dawns + Dusks*, p. 130.

2. Glimcher, op. cit., p. 74.

3. *Nevelson*. Colette Roberts. p. 16.

4. *Atmospheres and Environments*. Edward Albee. p. 57.

5. *Dawns + Dusks*, p. 122.

6. Ibid., p. 101.

7. Interview with Louise Nevelson, July 29, 1982.

8. Roberts, op. cit., p. 22.

9. Ibid.

10. *Dawns + Dusks*, p. 119.

11. Ibid., p. 127.

12. Ibid., p. 131.

13. Ibid., p. 133.

14. Roberts, op cit., p. 25.

Chapter Nine   "Queen of the Black Black"

1. Glimcher, op. cit., pp. 94, 95.

2. *Dawns + Dusks*, p. 138.

3. Roberts, op. cit., p. 24.

4. *Dawns + Dusks*, pp. 125–126.

5. Ibid., p. 145.

6. *Artnews*, September, 1961. Philip Pearlstein.

7. Quoted by Glimcher, op. cit., p. 101.

8. *Dawns + Dusks*, p. 138.

9. Ibid., p. 144.

10. Quoted in *Atmospheres and Environments*, p. 174, from: *Artnews*, January, 1960 (Thomas B. Hess).

11. Quoted by Glimcher, p. 108 from: Dore Ashton, "Louise Nevelson," *Climaise*, April–June, 1960.

Chapter Ten   Free To Be a Sensation

1. Glimcher, op. cit., p. 111.

2. *Dawns + Dusks*, p. 144.

3. Interview with Constance Schwartz, April 1, 1983.

4. *Dawns + Dusks*, p. 147.

5. Ibid., p. 184.

6. *Time*, January 12, 1981.

7. *Art Talk*, pp. 60–61. Cindy Nemser.

8. *Time*, January 12, 1981.

9. Arnold Glimcher interview with Louise Nevelson, January 30, 1972, Archives of American Art.

10. Carolyn Strickley, *Creative Crafts*, January–February, 1964.

11. Louise Nevelson talk at Museum of Fine Art, Roslyn, N.Y., February 23, 1983.

12. *New York Journal American*, September 4, 1965, p. 7.

Chapter Eleven   Adding New Dimensions

1. Glimcher, op. cit., pp. 153–155.
2. *Dawns + Dusks*, p. 163.
3. Ibid., p. 167.
4. Ibid., pp. 170–171.
5. *New York Times*, December 15,1972.
6. *Artnews*, May, 1979, p. 71.
7. *Dawns + Dusks*, p. 86.
8. *Newsweek*, December, 1977.
9. *Dawns + Dusks*, p. 81.
10. *Art Talk*, p. 63.
11. *Dawns + Dusks*, p. 64.
12. Ibid., p. 59.
13. Ted Streeter interview with Louise Nevelson, January 25, 1959, Archives of American Art.
14. *Dawns + Dusks*, p. 120.
15. Ibid., p. 43.
16. Ibid., p. 115.
17. Arnold Glimcher interview with Louise Nevelson, op. cit.
18. *Art Talk*, p. 55.
19. Interview with Louise Nevelson, July 29, 1982.
20. *Dawns + Dusks*, p. 115.
21. Ibid., p. 107.
22. Ibid., p. 115.
23. Louise Nevelson, talk at Cooper Union, November 22, 1982.
24. *Dawns + Dusks*, p. 115.

Chapter Twelve   The Search Continues

1. *New York Post*, January 17, 1976. (Quoted by Glimcher, *op. cit.*, p. 175)
2. Interview with Louise Nevelson, July 29, 1982.
3. *Artnews*, May 1979, p. 72.
4. Interview with Louise Nevelson, July 29, 1982.
5. Conversation with Ann Grinn, November 4, 1981.
6. Louise Nevelson talk at Museum of Fine Art, Roslyn, N.Y., February 23, 1983.
7. *Dawns + Dusks*, p. 167.
8. Laurie Wilson, *Fourth Dimension*, p. 11.
9. *New York Times*, April 27, 1980.
10. *Artnews*, May, 1979. (Diamonstein)
11. *Dawns + Dusks*, p. 168.
12. *New York Times*, April 27, 1980.
13. Louise Nevelson interview with Dorothy Seckler, May/June, 1964, Archives of American Art.
14. Louise Nevelson talk at Museum of Fine Art, Roslyn, N.Y., February 23, 1983.
15. Arnold Glimcher interview with Louise Nevelson, January 30, 1972, Archives of American Art.
16. Louise Nevelson talk at Museum of Fine Art, Roslyn, N.Y., February 23, 1983.
17. *Time*, January 12, 1981.
18. *New York Times* (Long Island Section), February 20, 1983. (Helen Harrison)
19. *Dawns + Dusks*, p. 69.
20. Ibid., p. 180.
21. Louise Nevelson, quoted in *Nature in Abstraction*, by John I. H. Baur, p. 76.

Bibliography

ABBOTT, BERENICE (text by Elizabeth McCausland). *New York in the Thirties*. New York: Dover Publications, Inc., 1973.

ALBEE, EDWARD (Introduction by). *Louise Nevelson: Atmospheres and Environments*. New York: Clarkson N. Potter, Inc. (Distributed by Crown Publishers, Inc. in association with the Whitney Museum of American Art, New York), 1980.

ANDERSON, JACK. *Dance*. New York: Newsweek Books, 1974.

ARNASON, H. H. *History of Modern Art*. New York: Harry N. Abrams, Inc. (no date).

BAIGELL, MATTHEW. *Dictionary of American Art*. New York: Harper & Row, 1979.

BAUR, JOHN I. H. *Nature in Abstraction*. New York: The Macmillan Company for the Whitney Museum of American Art, 1958.

DENBY, EDWIN. *Looking at the Dance*. New York: Horizon Press, 1949.

Encyclopedia Judaica. Jerusalem, Israel: Keter Publishing House Jerusalem, Ltd., 1972, Vol. 10.

GLIMCHER, ARNOLD B. *Louise Nevelson*. New York: E. P. Dutton & Co., Inc., 1976.

GUGGENHEIM, PEGGY. *Out of This Century*. New York: The Dial Press, 1946.

HARDEN, BRIAN R., ed. *Shore Village Album*. Rockland, Maine: The Shore Village Historical Society, 1977.

HARDEN, BRIAN R. *Shore Village Story*. Rockland, Maine: Rockland Bicentennial Commission/Courier-Gazette, 1976.

HARTT, FREDERICK. *A History of Painting, Sculpture, Architecture*, Volume II. New York: Harry N. Abrams, Inc., 1976.

HESCHEL, ABRAHAM JOSHUA. *The Earth is the Lord's*. New York: Farrar Straus & Giroux, 1977.

HOWE, IRVING. *World of Our Fathers*. New York: Simon & Schuster, 1976.

JANSON, H. W. *History of Art for Young People*. New York: Harry N. Abrams, Inc., 1982.

LARKIN, OLIVER W. *Art and Life in America*. New York: Rinehart & Company, Inc., 1949.

LASKY, KATHERINE. *The Night Journey*. Frederick Warne and Co., Inc., 1981.

MACKOWN, DIANA. *Dawns + Dusks*. New York: Charles Scribner's Sons, 1976.

NEMSER, CINDY. *Art Talk: Conversations with Twelve Women Artists*. New York: Charles Scribner's Sons, 1976.

PATTERSON, JERRY E. *The City of New York*. New York: Harry N. Abrams, Inc., 1978.

RABINOWITZ, SHALOM. *The Great Fair*. New York: Noonday Press, 1955.

ROBERTS, COLETTE. *Nevelson*. Paris: The Pocket Museum, Editions Georges Fall, 1964.

SADIE, STANLEY, ED. *The New Grove Dictionary of Music and Musicians*, Vol. 15. London: Macmillian Publishing, Ltd., 1980 (Norris, Geoffrey. "Rakhmaninov, Sergey." pp. 550–558)

SAMUEL, MAURICE. *The World of Sholom Aleichem*. New York: Schocken Books, 1965.

SAYLER, OLIVER M., ed. *Max Reinhardt and His Theatre*. New York: Brentano's, Inc., Publishers, 1924.

SHORES, LOUIS, ed. *Collier's Encyclopedia*, Vols. 11, 12, 16. New York: The Crowell-Collier Publishing Company, 1961.

WHITEHOUSE, ROGER. *New York: Sunshine and Shadow*. (a photographic record of the city and its people from 1850 to 1915) New York: Harper & Row, 1974.

Who's Who in American Art. New York: R. R. Bowker Company, 1980 (re: Ralph Rosenborg, p. 635)

WILSON, LAURIE. *Louise Nevelson: Iconography and Source*. New York: Garland Publishing, Inc., 1981. (Originally presented as Ph.D. thesis—City University of New York, 1978)

WPA *Guide to New York City: The Federal Writers Project Guide to 1930s New York*. New York: Pantheon Books, 1982.

ZBOROWSKI, MARK and HERZOG, ELIZABETH. *Life Is with People*. New York: Schocken Books, 1952.

CATALOGUES

BARO, GENE. *Nevelson: The Prints*. New York: Pace Editions, Inc., 1974.

DIAMONSTEIN, BARBARALEE. "Louise Nevelson: A Conversation with Barbaralee Diamonstein." *Nevelson: Maquettes for Monumental Sculpture*. New York: The Pace Gallery, 1980.

FDR *and the Arts: The WPA Arts Projects Exhibition in the New York Public Library*. 1983.

GORDON, JOHN. *Louise Nevelson*. New York: Whitney Museum of American Art, 1967.

KIESLER, FRIEDERICH. "Debacle of the Modern Theatre." *International Theatre Exposition*. New York, 1926.

MILLER, DOROTHY C., ed. *Sixteen Americans*. New York: The Museum of Modern Art, 1959.

Louise Nevelson. Rockland, Maine: William A. Farnsworth Library and Art Museum, 1979.

Louise Nevelson: The Fourth Dimension. Phoenix, Arizona: Phoenix Art Museum, 1980. (essay by Laurie Wilson)

Nevelson. New York: Martha Jackson Gallery, 1961. (Foreword by Kenneth Sawyer; poem by Jean Arp; commentary by Georges Mathieu)

Nevelson. New York: The Pace Gallery, 1964.

Nevelson: Sky Gates and Collages. New York: The Pace Gallery, 1974.

Peggy Guggenheim Collection, Venice. New York: Solomon R. Guggenheim Foundation, 1983.

SCHWARTZ, CONSTANCE. *Nevelson and O'Keeffe: Independents of the Twentieth Century*. Roslyn Harbor, New York: Nassau County Museum of Fine Art, 1983.

SHIREY, DAVID L. "Louise Nevelson." *Nevelson: Wood Sculpture and Collages*. New York: Wildenstein, 1980.

FILM

GRAHAM, MARTHA. A *Dancer's World* (1957). Film. Dance Division, New York Public Library.

MACKOWN, DIANA. Geometry and Magic: Louise Nevelson (1982). Ivon Crystal Films.

PERIODICALS

ADLMANN, JAN. "Rockland Artist's Work Captures World Acclaim at 31st Venice Biennale." *The Courier-Gazette*, Rockland, Maine, August 9, 1963.

ALBRIGHT, THOMAS. "Art is a Conviction—A Way of Life." *San Francisco Chronicle*, February 25, 1977.

BETHANY, M. "Sculptor's Environment." *New York Times Magazine*, April 27, 1980, pp. 132–136.

BICENTENNIAL ISSUE. *Courier-Gazette*. Rockland, Maine, March 20, 1976.

BONGARTZ, R. "I don't want to waste time, says Louise Nevelson at 70." *New York Times Magazine*, January 24, 1971, pp. 12–13, 30–34.

BRENSON, MICHAEL. "Art People." *New York Times*, Oct. 8, 1982, Sec. III, p. 21.

CANADAY, JOHN. "Louise Nevelson and the Rule Book." *New York Times*, April 6, 1969.

COUTTS-SMITH, KENNETH. "Nevelson." *The Arts Review*, London, November 16–30, 1963, p. 16.

DIAMONSTEIN, BARBARALEE. "Louise Nevelson: 'It takes a lot to tango.' " *Artnews*, May, 1979, pp. 69–72.

"Epic of Shoeshine Culture." *Newsweek*, January 4, 1943, p. 64.

FRIED, MICHAEL. "New York Letter." *Art International*, February, 1963, pp. 60–64.

GENAUER, EMILY. "A Scavenger's Black Magic." *New York World Journal Telegram* (magazine), March 12, 1967, p. 33.

GENT, GEORGE. "Sculptor Thanks the City in Steel." *New York Times*, December 15, 1972, p. 51.

GLUECK, GRACE. "Art People." *New York Times*, October 31, 1977.

GOLDBERG, VICKI. "Louise Nevelson." *Saturday Review*, August, 1980, pp. 34–37.

GOODMAN, CYNTHIA. "Friederich Kiesler: Designs for Peggy Guggenheim's Art of this Century Gallery." *Arts Magazine*, June, 1977, pp. 90–95.

GOODMAN, CYNTHIA. "Hans Hofmann as a Teacher." *Arts*, April, 1979, pp. 120–125.

GREENBERG, CLEMENT. "America Takes the Lead, 1945–1965." *Art in America*, August-September, 1965, pp. 108–109.

HARNETT, LILA. "Louise Nevelson's World." *Cue*, December 10–23, 1977. pp. 19–20.

HARRISON, HELEN A. "O'Keeffe and Nevelson Works In Rare Juxtaposition." *The New York Times*, February 20, 1983 (Sunday, Long Island Section).

HORAN, ROBERT. "The Recent Theatre of Martha Graham." *Dance Index*, New York, January, 1947.

HUGHES, ROBERT. "Night and Silence, Who Is There?" *Time*, December 12, 1977, pp. 59–60.

KISSELGOFF, ANNA. "How Dance and Other Arts Influence Each Other." *New York Times*, January 16, 1983, p. 24 H.

KRAMER, HILTON. "Month in Review." *Arts*, February, 1959, pp. 48–51.

KRAMER, HILTON. "Nevelson's Dazzling Feats." *New York Times*, May 11, 1980, Section 2, pp. 1, 30–31.

MARTIN, JOHN. "The Dance: Noguchi." *New York Times*, February 29, 1948, section 2, p. 3.

MC COY, GARNETT. "Poverty, Politics and Artists 1930–1945." *Art in America*, August-September, 1965, pp. 88–107. (from *The Artist Speaks*, presented by the Archives of American Art).

NAPPI, LOU. "Great Contributions to Surrealist Art, Says Noted Woman Sculptor of Joe Milone's Odd Shoe-Shine Box." *Corriere D'America*, New York: January 10, 1943.

NEVELSON, LOUISE. "Art At The Flatbush Boys Club." *Flatbush Magazine*, June, 1935. p. 3.

NEVELSON, LOUISE, "Queen of the Black Black." In Philip Pearlstein, "The Private Myth." *Artnews*, September, 1961, pp. 42–45.

NEVELSON, LOUISE. "The Sculptor." *Newsweek*, July 4, 1976, p. 53.

NOCKLIN, LINDA. 'Why Have There Been No Great Women Artists?" and Nevelson, Louise, "Do Your Work." *Artnews*, January, 1971, pp. 22–45.

N.Y. *Journal-American*, September 4, 1965, p. 7.

PERLMAN, BARABARA, "At 79, she is busier than ever." *Scottsdale (Arizona) Daily Progress*, March 31, 1978, pp. 50–52.

PRICE, REYNOLDS. "The Heroes of Our Times." *Saturday Review*, December, 1978, pp. 16–29.

RILEY, MAUDE. "Irrepressible Nevelson." *Art Digest*, April 15, 1943.

SAWIN, MARTICA. "The Achievement of Ralph Rosenborg." *Arts*, November, 1960, pp. 44–47.

SCHWARTZ, ELLEN. "Two From Nevelson: A stunning chapel and a place for the child in all of us." *Artnews*, February, 1978, pp. 54–55.

SEIBERLING, DOROTHY. "Weird Woodword of Lunar World." *Life*, March 24, 1958, pp. 77–80.

SMITH, CHARLES C. "The Sculpture Factory." *Boston Sunday Globe*, August 27, 1975, pp. 21, 35.

STEVENS, MARK. "The Wood Witch." *Newsweek*, December 19, 1977, pp. 95–96.

STRICKLER, CAROLYN, "Interview with Louise Nevelson." *Creative Crafts*, January/February, 1964, pp. 2–4.

Washington Post, July 7, 1963.

WILBUR, ALINE. "In 'pursuit of fleeting shadows.' " *Christian Science Monitor*, May 16, 1974.

WILSON, LAURIE. "Bride of the Black Moon: An Iconographic Study of the Work of Louise Nevelson." *Arts*, May, 1980, pp. 140–148.

World Telegram and Sun, September 22, 1964.

Miscellaneous uncatalogued material, including interviews, correspondence, photos, sketches, lists, catalogues, articles, clippings and press releases:

1) Archives of American Art
2) William A. Farnsworth Library and Art Museum Archives
3) Museum of Modern Art Library
4) Museum of the City of New York
5) New York Public Library of the Performing Arts
6) Whitney Museum of American Art Library
7) Yivo Institute for Jewish Studies

INTERVIEWS WITH THE AUTHOR

Louise Nevelson, New York
    October 28, 1981
    July 29, 1982
    February 23, 1983
    February 25, 1983
    telephone—March 17, 1982
            April 13, 1983
Anita Weinstein, Rockland, Maine
    March 23, 1982
    letter dated January 13, 1983
Constance Schwartz, New York
    April 1, 1983
Louise Nevelson—talks:
    at Cooper Union, N.Y., November 22, 1982
    at Museum of Fine Art, Roslyn, N.Y., February 23, 1983

Louise Nevelson
Exhibits and Works
Mentioned

Index